Arnold Palmer

Arnold Palmer

A TRIBUTE TO AN AMERICAN ICON

DAVID FISCHER
AND DAVID ARETHA

Skyhorse Publishing

Skyhorse Publishing books may be purchased in bulk at special discounts for sales promotion, corporate gifts, fund-raising, or educational purposes. Special editions can also be created to specifications. For details, contact the Special Sales Department, Skyhorse Publishing, 307 West 36th Street, 11th Floor, New York, NY 10018 or info@skyhorsepublishing.com.

Skyhorse® and Skyhorse Publishing® are registered trademarks of Skyhorse Publishing, Inc.®, a Delaware corporation.

Visit our website at www.skyhorsepublishing.com.

10 9 8 7 6 5 4 3 2 1

Library of Congress Cataloging-in-Publication Data is available on file.

Cover design by Tom Lau
Cover photos: AP Images

Print ISBN: 978-1-5107-2485-3
Ebook ISBN: 978-1-5107-2486-0

Printed in China

To Arnie (of course!).

Thank you for the thrills and inspiration, for your kindness and generosity.

Golf is a better game, and the world a better place, because of you.

CONTENTS

PREFACE

"THE EVERYDAY MAN'S HERO"

Most of us remember Arnold Palmer as a kindly gentleman, the uncle or grandpa we wished we had. Though he moved slowly in older age, he warmed our hearts with his sunset smile and small-town charm. Perhaps we recall a hunched Arnie traversing Hogan Bridge at Augusta National at his 50th Masters, waving his visor one last time. Or wearing Sansabelt slacks and a yellow golf shirt at Latrobe in an '80s Pennzoil commercial, saying, "You know, this old tractor and I are a lot alike." Or, if we're old enough to remember the '70s, we might recall him clutching an iron to his midsection and mouthing an "owww" while his approach shot hooks into the trees.

But long before he became lovable ol' Arnie, Palmer took the golf world by storm with a youthful exuberance—a controlled recklessness. Slender and schoolboy handsome with powerful arms, smiling confidently and effusing energy, Arnold drove the green, went for broke, and "charged" down the stretch of major tournaments, captivating galleries along the way. Sam Snead said that every time Palmer drove the ball, it looked like he was trying to hole his tee

shot. "He wasn't far off the mark," Arnie replied. Instead of chipping out of the woods after a drive gone awry, he found a clearing in the trees and blasted toward the green. Sometimes he failed; sometimes he made it. Either way, Arnie's Army applauded the effort. "Arnold Palmer," Jack Nicklaus said, "was the everyday man's hero."

Palmer was not a young phenom like Tiger Woods or an age-defier like Snead or Nicklaus. He won 44 PGA Tour events in his 30s (1959–69), the most by any player in history. And though many of us remember him as old Uncle Arnie who struggled in the '70s and beyond, a competitive fire burned within him long after his glory days were over.

Case in point: the 1980 Masters. Palmer hadn't won on Tour in seven years, and he had failed to break 70 at Augusta in his last 18 rounds there. But for Sunday's round, he was paired with Nicklaus, his friendly, fierce, and much younger rival of 20 years. "Arnie plays better when he's got something like this to light his fire," said his wife, Winnie. Or, as Palmer said when he learned of the Sunday pairing, "I'll whip his ass." Arnie, age 50, went out and shot a 69 to Jack's 73.

Arnold Palmer obliges his ever-present army with autographs before the opening round of the U.S. Open at Pebble Beach, California, on June 16, 1982. (AP Photo/Jim Palmer)

While most sports stars are revered from afar, Palmer engaged with the fans in a warm, personable, respectful manner.

As Raymond Floyd said, Palmer "set the standard for how superstars in every sport ought to be, in the way he has always signed autographs, in the way he has always made time for everyone. On the golf course, all I ever saw was a mass of people. He was able to focus in on everyone in the gallery individually. It wasn't fake.

"And man, could he play the game."

Though they called him "The King," Arnold remained forever humble. When he returned to the links after recovering from prostate cancer, he downplayed the comeback. "I'm not interested in being a hero," he said. "I just want to play some golf."

If you're an older reader, we hope this book rekindles memories of Arnie's magical moments.

If you're a younger reader, be prepared to be inspired.

INTRODUCTION

GOING FOR BROKE

Full of vigor and self-assurance, Arnold Palmer stepped to the par-4 1st hole of Cherry Hills Country Club and attempted to drive the green. It was the first round of the 1960 U.S. Open, and the young-at-heart basher felt he could blast onto the putting surface of the 346-yard hole. Sure, balls travel farther in the high altitude of Englewood, Colorado, but perhaps the thin air also affected his brain.

Palmer swung out of his shoes and didn't come close to the green. Instead, the ball sliced into the trees on the right and fell into a fast-running stream. Arnold looked over at USGA Executive Director Joe Dey. "Joe," Arnold quipped, "I think I'll just let that run on down to the green." Dey scrunched up his face and replied, "Now Arnold, you know better than that." Instead, Palmer retrieved the ball from the ditch, dropped it, and made a double-bogey 6. His attempt to "go for broke" on Cherry Hills No. 1 had been a terrible mistake.

Back in 1960, the U.S. Open was indeed played on Father's Day weekend, but not on Father's Day. Round 1 took place on Thursday, Round 2 was held on Friday, and the final two rounds—a grueling 36 holes—were staged on Saturday. Prior to the morning and afternoon rounds on Saturday, players ate cheeseburgers (apparently the best source of energy at the time), drank iced teas, and chatted with colleagues and reporters.

"Well, that burned me up. I was so hot that I couldn't finish my hamburger." —Arnold Palmer prior to the final round of the 1960 U.S. Open, after being told by Bob Drum that he couldn't win even if he finished with a 65

During that mid-round break, not many golf writers wanted to talk to Palmer. He was too far back. Despite winning five PGA Tour events already in 1960, including the Masters—and despite 20 Tour victories since debuting in 1954—Palmer sat at 15th on the leader board, seven strokes back, entering the final round. Instead, much of the buzz

Palmer lifts an iron shot during a 1962 event. "Everybody talks about how he had this unorthodox swing, but it was only the finish that was unorthodox," said instructor Hank Haney. "He was so solid through the ball." (AP Images/Ted Powers)

centered on leader Mike Souchak, a rugged former Duke University placekicker who held the lead at five-under.

But in that clubhouse, and across America as sports fans tuned in on television, most of the focus centered on an aging legend and an up-and-coming superstar. Paired together for the final round, Ben Hogan and Jack Nicklaus stood at three-under. Hogan, the 47-year-old "Iceman," had won a record-tying four U.S. Opens, including three after a near-fatal car crash in 1949 that wreaked havoc on his legs. A scholar of the game and a perfect ball-striker, Hogan now struggled only with his putting—and perhaps his stamina. Commentators suggested that his ravaged legs wouldn't carry him through 36 holes on Saturday.

The stern-faced Hogan found his match in countenance with Nicklaus. A 20-year-old Ohio State student, Nicklaus was a burly amateur. Someone suggested that he looked like a German bus driver. "Jack Nicklaus," comedian Don Rickles would quip, "he's a real live wire." At the time, Nicklaus was so unknown in the mainstream that a newsreel narrator the next week would refer to him as "Jack Nick-louse." Nevertheless, Jack's talent was monstrous, and reporters wondered if he'd become the first post-Depression amateur to win the U.S. Open.

As for Palmer, the odds of him leapfrogging 14 competitors and erasing a seven-stroke deficit seemed so preposterous that only *he* was thinking about it. In the locker room prior to his 1:42 start time for the final round, Palmer chatted with a half-interested Bob Drum of the *Pittsburgh Press*, who had been covering Palmer since his days as an amateur out of Latrobe Country Club. Fellow sportswriter Dan Jenkins, in the room at the time, recalled the exchange in his book *Fairways and Greens*:

> "If I drive the green and get a birdie or an eagle, I might shoot sixty-five," Palmer said. "What'll that do?"
> Drum said, "Nothing. You're too far back."
> "It would give me two-eighty," Palmer said. "Doesn't two-eighty always win the Open?"
> "Yeah, when Hogan shoots it," I said, laughing heartily at my own wit.

According to Jenkins, Drum saw Palmer lingering around the doorway and shooed him out. "Go on, boy," Drum said, according to Jenkins. "Get out of here. Go make your seven or eight birdies but shoot seventy-three. I'll see you later."

Palmer was good friends with Drum and familiar with his irascible sense of humor, but Drum's dismissiveness in the locker room really pissed him off—or, as Arnie put it, "burned me up." When he stepped outside, he vowed to prove those doubters wrong. While known for his "charges," Palmer would have to outdo himself. In fact, he would have to stage the greatest comeback in U.S. Open history.

As he stood perched on the elevated 1st tee, with sun glimmering off snow-capped mountains in the backdrop, Palmer waggled his driver with his mighty arms. Not only had he failed to drive the 1st green on Thursday, but he had also fallen short in the same attempt the two previous rounds—not a good thing considering the high weeds that fronted the putting surface, the penalty for all fence-swinging failures.

Palmer, with his go-get-'em attitude, took a mighty rip. "I hit it as hard as I could," he recalled, "and it had a good trajectory, and it carried to the front fringe and bounced on."

Incredibly, with only half a cheeseburger in his belly, Palmer had blasted the ball 339 of the 346 yards. "The crowd went crazy," Cherry Hills member Sue Chamlee told Golf.com decades later. "We just screamed when it went on the green. It still excites me."

Palmer said he was so excited that he almost three-putted, but he made the second putt for a birdie. On the 2nd hole, he thrilled the gallery again when he chipped in from 90 feet for another birdie. In living rooms across the

Time's May 2, 1960, cover story described Palmer as having "strength in all the right places: massive shoulders and arms, a waist hardly big enough to hold his trousers up, thick wrists, and leather-hard, outsized hands that can crumple a beer can as though it were tissue paper." (Authors' Collection)

country, golf fans were nudging their buddies: Souchak's ahead, but watch out for Palmer!

In 1960, a youthful spirit was in the air. The youngest of the Baby Boomers, born in 1946, were ushering in the first teen-dominated culture. Moreover, after eight years of doughty Dwight and Mamie Eisenhower, Americans eagerly awaited the young and dynamic John and Jacqueline Kennedy.

And at Cherry Hills on this late-spring afternoon, amid the serious mugs of his competitors, Palmer stood out as a fresh face. He wasn't young (age 30), but he seemed like it. His smooth skin, apple cheeks, and easy smile endeared him to the galleries. His light brown hair, though receding, twirled up in the front, like soft-serve ice cream. Really, he looked like a character out of the Archie comic books that were popular at the time.

If Palmer's cheery face didn't win over the young ladies—as well as their mothers—then surely his strapping physique did, namely his slim waist and bulging biceps. And he was charming too—as polite as *Leave It to Beaver's* Eddie Haskell, with none of the insincerity.

Dressed in light slacks, a white golf shirt, and a white visor, Palmer continued his quest to prove Drum wrong. On the 348-yard par-4 3rd hole, he tried to drive the green again. The drive went into the trees instead, but after a crowd-rousing approach that he nearly sank, he made birdie. He birdied the 4th hole with an 18-foot putt and in fact birdied six of the first seven. "On the 8th hole," Arnie told Golf.com, "here comes Drum, walking down the fairway with all the press corps. I remember looking at him—I was still pissed off—and I said, 'What are you doing out here?' And they all laughed."

"It was such a charge," eyewitness Bob Warren told KDVR.com, "and he was famous for that charge and the army ["Arnie's Army"], and everybody was caught up in the excitement and everyone was like, 'Here he goes again!'"

In 1960, Americans cheered wholesome male heroes who triumphed over all comers: Johnny Unitas, Mickey Mantle, Perry Mason, and Marshal Dillon in *Gunsmoke*. Now, as Arnie burned through Cherry Hills with a 30 on the front nine, exciting the gallery with his comeback spirit, TV viewers could add Arnold Palmer to the list.

**"Golf was a sleepy country club game, and then along comes this muscular, tilting Pennsylvanian with a corkscrew swing and a handsome grimace, and suddenly he was an irresistible figure."
—Jim Dodson, Palmer biographer**

Arnie shot one-under 35 on the back nine, giving him a 65—a new U.S. Open record for the final round. In fact, that number, along with his final 280, were the scores that he had suggested to Drum and Jenkins. While Nicklaus would finish in second place at 282, Hogan had a chance to prevail as late as the 71st hole. But after his approach spun back off the green and

Arnold prepares to toss his visor after sinking his par putt on 18 in the final round of the 1960 U.S. Open. He birdied seven and bogeyed one of the first 11 holes, then parred the last seven to achieve his famous 65. (AP Photo)

into a water hazard that fronted it, and after Hogan triple-bogeyed the 18th, Arnold Palmer was the U.S. Open champion.

An elated Palmer jokes with Jack Nicklaus after defeating the 20-year-old amateur by two strokes at the 1960 U.S. Open. Jack would avenge the loss by slaying Palmer in a 1962 U.S. Open playoff. (AP Photo)

Writer Dan Jenkins snarkily told Palmer that a four-under 280 wouldn't be enough to win the 1960 U.S. Open, but Arnie—who shot a 65 in the final round—proved him wrong. (AP Photo)

Earlier, after his final putt, Arnie flung his visor toward the gallery—an iconic moment in golf history. "Oh my God, the whole place erupted," Warren recalled.

Golf had long been a "gentlemen's" sport, one reliant on decorum and etiquette, with polite clapping and the occasional *shushing* that dampened enthusiasm. Arnold Palmer shattered the stereotype with his go-for-broke style and magnetic personality—and it all coincided with the rise of television. "Arnold popularized the game," Nicklaus said. "He gave it a shot in the arm when the game needed it."

America mourned the loss of "The King" on September 25, 2016, when Palmer died at age 87. Three days later, his ashes were spread over Latrobe, Pennsylvania—the town where his legend began.

CHAPTER 1

DEACON'S BOY

Arnold Palmer set out for the Western Pennsylvania Junior Championship at Highland Country Club about six miles north of Pittsburgh ready to take on the world. It was 1946, and the cock-sure 17-year-old from nearby Latrobe was feeling confident. Why shouldn't he? Arnold was the Pennsylvania high school champion, and he had been collecting amateur circuit trophies like other boys his age collected baseball cards. Arnold Palmer was surely on the come.

When he arrived in Pittsburgh, however, tournament officials turned Arnold away. His entry form was denied because his home base, Latrobe Country Club, was not a member of the Western Pennsylvania Golf Association. Distraught, Arnold begged his father, Deacon, the golf professional at Latrobe, to pull some strings. Deacon reluctantly contacted a fellow pro at a club that *was* a member of the WPGA to call in a favor for his son. The younger Palmer was made a WPGA member on the spot. Now eligible to compete, Arnold played the Highland course with purpose and precision, fueled by his desire to rectify any perceived personal slight.

An incident occurred in Pittsburgh on that day that had a lasting impact on how Arnold approached and played the game. It happened somewhere on Highland's back nine. Arnold was protecting a slim lead, and he was on the green preparing to make par. He missed a short putt, and in frustration he turned and hurled his putter in disgust. The putter flew like a whirligig over the gallery of fans, landing in some small trees beyond the fringe. Though Arnold would regain his composure and go on to post a dramatic final-hole victory, his jubilation of claiming another shiny new trophy quickly waned on the car ride home. During the 50-mile drive, he never heard a word of congratulations from his father, only a deafening, stony silence. Back home in Latrobe, Arnold's father finally let his son have it.

"If you ever throw a club like that again," Deacon Palmer said, "you'll never play in another golf tournament."

Deacon Palmer's son never threw a golf club in anger again.

***

Arnold Daniel Palmer was born in Youngstown, Pennsylvania, on September 10, 1929—seven weeks before

East Main Street, looking West,
Latrobe, Pa.

Deacon Palmer arrived in Latrobe in 1921, several years after this photo was taken, to help build a golf course. The house in which Arnold grew up in the 1930s was a far cry from these idyllic homes along East Main Street. (Authors' Collection)

the stock market crashed and burned. He grew up in Latrobe, a small working-class town with three steel mills in the foothills of the Allegheny Mountains, located in the western part of the state. Deacon and Doris Palmer paid $15 a month in rent for a cozy two-story white frame house. Arnold was the oldest of four children. A sister, Lois Jean, was born 21 months later. Cheech, as she was called, was close to her big brother. A brother, Jerry, and another sister, Sandy, arrived 15 and 19 years after Arnold's birth.

> **"[Latrobe] isn't just where I came from and where I grew up, but it's the home that's in my heart. If there's one thing I've learned in all these years, it's this: your hometown is not where you're from, but it's who you are."**
> **—Arnold Palmer**

Deacon, Doris, Arnold, and Cheech made do without indoor plumbing, using an outhouse located out back near a maintenance shed. What made the house special was that it sat about 50 yards off the 6th tee at the Latrobe Country Club, a nine-hole course where Deacon worked as the groundskeeper and teaching pro for 45 years until his death in 1976.

As a young man of 17, Deacon Palmer helped create the Latrobe Country Club with his bare hands, literally digging ditches as a member of the construction crew that built the place. When it was finished in 1921, he was asked to stay on and help maintain the course. He never left. Everyone at Latrobe knew Deacon—they called him Deke—but Arnold always called his old man Pap. Arnold followed Pap around the golf course, where he learned the virtues of hard work and the importance of following the rules. Deacon Palmer was a tough-love disciplinarian. He never let his son forget that he wasn't a member's kid; he was an employee's kid. That meant boundaries. Arnold couldn't swim in the pool while members were present or play golf until the final foursome had completed their rounds. Arnold came from

This postcard captures a downtown street in Latrobe in the 1950s. Arnold preferred to spend his time in the more rural part of town. (Authors' Collection)

modest means, raised by parents who taught him to mind his place in the social order. The young master Palmer never forgot that he was the one on the outside looking in.

Arnold first started playing golf with a cut-off shortened hickory-shaft brassie (today's equivalent of a 2-wood) and an old iron with a sawed-off shaft given to him by his father. Deacon insisted on teaching his three-year-old son the classic Vardon grip, which involves overlapping the small finger of one hand on the index finger of the other, at an age when Arnold could barely tie his own shoelaces. "I vividly remember swinging the club hours at a time as Pap and his men worked nearby," he told the *Saturday Evening Post* in 1960.

Palmer works on his clubs in the basement of his home in Latrobe on May 23, 1962. He learned the tools of the trade as a boy by working in the pro shop at Latrobe Country Club. (AP Photo)

"I'd be swinging at some remote spot on the course, and my dad would walk by and tell me what I was doing wrong. I would correct myself and start swinging some more."

Arnold's father impressed on him the importance of keeping a firm hold on the club and not letting the swing get too loose. Even as a kid Arnold had a compact swing. He tried to hit the ball so hard he often would lose his balance. Deacon wanted it that way. Father instructed son not to complicate matters. Deacon advised him to identify a target, aim, and fire.

"Hit it hard, boy," he said simply. "Go find it and hit it hard again."

Arnold never did it any other way.

***

The game of golf came easily to Arnold. By the time he was eight, he was earning pocket change by standing at the 6th tee and offering to drive the ladies' balls over a drainage ditch that crossed the fairway 120 yards away (so that they wouldn't hit the balls into the ditch) for a nickel a pop. On a good day he would earn 30 cents to spend on ice cream and a movie. As for school, Arnold was an average student, but his main concern was finishing his homework quickly enough so he could go work on his game. Unlike the other kids in Latrobe, Arnold didn't much care about team sports. Playing golf was all he wanted to do. He hit practice shots at every available opportunity. Weather was never an obstacle. In winter, Arnold painted the white golf balls red so he could drive them into the snow, find them,

and hit them again. Soon he was hitting the golf ball harder and farther than anyone his age had a right to hit it.

As Deacon's son, he got to play the course later in the day, once the members had gone home. He played nearly every evening and covered as many holes as daylight allowed. In time, he knew the course like the back of his own hand. At eight, he could shoot 55 for nine holes. Then he got it down to 50. One day, when he was nine, he shot even 5s for a 45. He couldn't wait to run home and tell his mother.

"Did you count them all?" she asked.

She and Pap never wanted their son to get a big head. Doris worked part-time as the club's bookkeeper. She called her son Fella. Deacon and Doris Palmer were opposites when it came to on-course parenting. Doris was the proud mother, letting everyone within earshot know that the boy with the powerful swing belonged to her. According to Arnold, no aspiring golfer ever had a more nurturing golf mom. Deacon, by contrast, watched his son play from a safe distance, inconspicuous in the crowd and pacing far behind the gallery ropes.

From the beginning Pap drilled into his son the idea that a golf course was a place where true character is revealed, both its strengths and weaknesses. Arnold was schooled on the rules and traditions that made golf the most gentlemanly game on earth. As a result, he learned to treat the golf course with respect. Because he knew what it took to maintain a golf course, he knew the importance of replacing divots and repairing spike marks. From his mother, he learned to congratulate an opponent after a good shot.

As a young caddie, Arnold played the Latrobe course after members had gone home. He covered as many holes as daylight allowed, honing his distinctive swing, seen here in Palm Springs, California, on February 27, 1967. (AP Photo)

> **"My father had polio as a child that left him with a pronounced limp. He wore a brace for as long as I could remember on his left leg. He compensated for this handicap by building up his upper body. He could do several one-handed pull-ups at a time with either hand. My father was tough, and he was smart."—Arnold Palmer**

Arnold's preteen world spanned only as far and wide as the fairways of Latrobe Country Club. But on the afternoon of December 7, 1941, the world changed. He'd just finished hitting practice balls and had come inside the pro shop to warm up. From the radio he heard that the Japanese had bombed Pearl Harbor. In the summer of '42, when so many men were off fighting in World War II, the club was short on labor. Deke needed his son to pitch in. Arnold began spending full days at the course, mowing fairways and greens in the morning, working in the pro shop in the afternoon, and carrying members' bags in between. Arnold built up his muscular arms by slinging heavy bags and by pushing his father's mowers around Latrobe's fairways. Soon he was overpowering the nine-hole, par-34 Latrobe course.

When he was old enough, Arnold, 11, had begun caddying for members at the club—more for the access to the course it allowed him than to actually make money. In the ensuing years, as Arnold's game took shape, he played out dramatic U.S. Open finishes in his imagination. He read instructional golf books and biographies of his golf heroes, Bobby Jones in particular, and began to dream about one day playing golf for a living. Mondays were the best days, because the club was closed and the caddies had their run of the place. The other boys would pretend to be their golfing heroes, imagining themselves as Walter Hagen, Gene Sarazen, or Byron Nelson as they stood over their ball. Not the groundskeeper's son. "I'm Arnold Palmer," he'd brazenly say every time. The other caddies marveled at Arnold's self-confidence and the faith he had in his own abilities. Golf will be my ticket out of Latrobe, Arnold told them; he just couldn't say where the sport would take him.

***

In the summer of 1943, while the World War raged overseas, peaceful Latrobe was buzzing in anticipation of a visit from one of the greatest athletes in the world. Still seven years away from sweeping all three events of the women's Grand Slam, Babe Didrikson Zaharias, who won three medals in track and field at the 1932 Olympics, was coming to town to put on a golfing exhibition. As impressed as Arnold was with her golf skills, it was her showmanship that dazzled him. With a large crowd around her, Babe stepped to the 1st tee, pegged up her ball, turned to the gallery, and announced, "Ladies and gentlemen, hold on for a second while I loosen my girdle." She then proceeded to blast the ball a country mile straight down the fairway. The crowd roared its approval, and Arnold was clearly drawn to the public admiration

A teenage Palmer, left, poses with two teammates from his Latrobe High School golf team in the 1940s. Arnold was the state champ as a junior in 1946 and repeated the feat the following year. (*Pittsburgh Post-Gazette*)

Babe received. For the first time, he became aware of his own desire to show off and please people in that manner. Babe had the flair for the spectacular and the talent to pull it off, and Arnold thought he did too. Prior to that, the only person Arnold wanted to please with his golf shots was his father, but after watching Babe do her thing, it occurred to him how great it would be to hear total strangers *oohing* and *aahing* over his golf shots.

Arnold experienced the thrill of wowing a gallery while winning the state's high school championship in 1946. His ball wound up in the rough behind a row of trees at the old course at Penn State. The trees were too tall to hit the ball over, so Arnold had to find another way. He picked a narrow gap between the trees and focused on the space, blocking out everything else. He hit the ball hard with a 5-iron, and it shot right through the gap and skipped onto the green. The crowd roared, and Arnold felt empowered all the way down to his toes. He took his cues from the crowd that day, and went for the pin with any club from anywhere on the course. With a club in his hand, Arnold was as refined as a raging bull. The crowd didn't care that he wasn't a stylist in the mold of Bobby Jones or Sam Snead. They loved Arnold's go-for-broke approach. The better and bolder his shots, the louder the crowd cheered him on.

As Arnold's knowledge of the game grew, so did his body. Physically, he was armed with broad shoulders, a barrel chest, big biceps, muscular, Popeye-like forearms, a flat stomach, and hips too narrow to hold up his pants. His skin was tan from a life in the sun. With hands that grew larger and stronger than his father's, he used them like a vise around the grip of a club. When he swung, always from the heels, it was like unleashing a tornado. Arnold's homemade swing—once likened to a man wrestling a snake—was a violent corkscrew motion that relied almost exclusively on upper-body strength.

"Deke is ruining that boy," some club members would say while watching Arnold nearly come out of his shoes. "He should make the kid swing easy."

The first real set of golf clubs Arnold used to learn the game as a teenager in the 1940s. The set is comprised of seven First Flight hickory-shaft irons and two Louisville woods. (Heritage Auctions)

Pap never let the criticism bother him. He cautioned Arnold never to alter his unorthodox swing.

"It'll work out all right as you get older," he told his son.

Arnold heeded his father's advice and refused to let anyone tinker with his mechanics. Deacon taught him that as long as he could hit the ball straight he'd have a big advantage over opponents. So Arnold worked on doing just that. Arnold always gave his father—who was the only golf instructor he ever had—much of the credit for his success.

***

Arnold was the No. 1 player on the golf team at Latrobe High School for four years. He lost only one match, to a senior when he was a freshman. He won two Pennsylvania high school state championships, three West Penn Junior titles, and five West Penn Amateurs. He made the semifinals of the Pennsylvania Amateur Championship as a high school senior. That year, he received an invitation to play as a wild card in his first pro tour event, the Dapper Dan Open, in Pittsburgh. "I wrecked my father's car going to the tournament," Arnold said, "and I didn't make the cut. But I got cut when I got home."

By the summer of 1947, around the time Arnold finished high school, he qualified to play in the Hearst National Junior Championship, in Los Angeles. He rode the train westward with Bud Worsham, a golfing acquaintance he knew from the amateur circuit. Bud was the younger brother of Lew Worsham, the pro at famed Oakmont and winner of the 1947 U.S. Open just a few weeks earlier. Arnold wanted to talk

Palmer as a senior at Latrobe High School in 1947. (*Pittsburgh Post-Gazette*)

about Lew's exciting playoff win over Sam Snead, but Bud wasn't biting. The whole way west to California, a two-day train ride, Bud talked up a storm about where he was going to college. Bud had a full scholarship to play golf at Wake Forest. He described a place down south in North Carolina where you could play golf all winter long and never interrupt your game on account of the cold weather. That sounded good to Arnold.

The truth was, Arnold hadn't really given much thought to going to college. Thanks to his impressive schoolboy press clippings, Palmer received interest from Penn State and the University of Pittsburgh, both offering full-tuition scholarships but not one penny for room and board. His Pap certainly couldn't afford to pay for his food and lodging elsewhere. With a houseful of hungry mouths to feed, Pap had a tough enough time trying to keep Arnold sated much less finance his son's college education. Arnold told Bud he was considering joining the Army, to get his military service out of the way. World War II was over, but the draft was still very much in business. As the train headed over the rails to the Hearst tournament, Bud came up with a bright idea. Maybe he could help Arnold by convincing the Wake Forest athletic director to give Arnold a full-ride golf scholarship like he himself had gotten. Bud called the school from California, and Arnold called his mother and asked her to hurriedly send his high school transcripts to Wake Forest, a place he knew nothing about except it was somewhere in North Carolina and sounded like heaven.

Palmer, circa 1947. (*Pittsburgh Post-Gazette*)

"When I was in college, I thought about becoming an attorney. But I wasn't smart enough; I hate being cooped up indoors; and I'm too nice a guy."—Arnold Palmer

Understandably distracted, Arnold did not fare well at the Hearst tournament; he was eliminated in the first round. But his disappointment at being knocked out early was quickly tempered by a letter he received a few days after he got home. It was a note from Wake Forest offering him the same full scholarship deal as Bud Worsham got. In September 1947, Arnold Palmer excitedly made preparations to follow his friend to Wake Forest. Though Arnold had never before been south of the Pennsylvania state line, now there was no question as to which direction he was heading.

CHAPTER 2

"THE EARTH SHAKES"

With golf his main pursuit, but majoring in business administration, Arnold Palmer entered Wake Forest in September 1947. Bud Worsham was his roommate. Buddy quickly became Arnold's best friend and running mate. The duo led a once feckless Demon Deacon squad to three consecutive Southern Conference championships. Arnold was Wake's best golfer, and he regularly beat the big-name players at the big-name golfing schools—like Art Wall and Mike Souchak of Duke—competitors he would later face on the pro tour.

Because Arnold was always yakking and boasting, some opponents called him Crow. He talked a good game and had the skills to back it up, winning both the 1949 and 1950 Southern Conference and NCAA individual titles. He predicted he would beat North Carolina's Harvie Ward in the 1950 conference championship and then went out and did just that. The Associated Press story in newspapers the next day called Arnold "the Wake Forest muscle man."

Arnold was making a name for himself, but his time at Wake Forest was cut short by a horrific tragedy. In the fall

Arnold Palmer burst on the scene at Wake Forest and quickly became the Demon Deacons' number-one player. Here he chips out of a trap during the Azalea Festival tournament in Wilmington, North Carolina, on March 27, 1954. (AP Images/Rudolph Faircloth)

of 1950, Buddy Worsham was killed in a car crash during a road trip to Durham, North Carolina. Arnold had been invited to go along but declined, having already agreed to go to the movies with another friend. The police took Arnold to the hospital to identify Buddy's body.

Arnold was devastated by the loss.

"Wake without Bud was unthinkable," he said.

Unable to cope, and in a heartbroken fog, he quit college during his senior year.

"I was mentally and physically and every other way shaken by the fact Buddy was killed," he would later recount, "and I realized life can have a destiny and you sometimes can't control that."

Looking for a temporary escape following Buddy's death, Palmer joined the United States Coast Guard and signed up for a three-year hitch. The only action he saw during the Korean War was the side bets he wagered on domestic golf courses. Arnold was stationed at Cape May, New Jersey, and then transferred to Connecticut, and then to Cleveland. While stationed there, Palmer won two Ohio Amateur titles. He left the service, decided to make golf a priority, and set out to conquer the world. In January 1954, he returned to Wake Forest and promptly reestablished himself as collegiate golf's dominant force by winning the inaugural Atlantic Coast Conference championship. He stayed at Wake Forest only one semester and left before completing his degree.

Palmer left college without a diploma, but with a singular mission. He was obsessed with becoming a better player than his hero, Bobby Jones. He set his sights on winning

Yeoman Arnold Palmer, 23, played in the North and South Amateur championship at Pinehurst Country Club in Pinehurst, North Carolina, in April 1953. Arnold was on leave from his duties in the 9th District Auxiliary office. (U.S. Coast Guard, courtesy of Wikimedia Commons)

Arnold drives for Wake Forest during the Southern Intercollegiate tournament at Athens, Georgia, in April 1954. Soon after, he left school to focus on his game. (AP Photo)

the U.S. Amateur championship, which he saw as a springboard to greater things. If he could win the national amateur championship, perhaps he could win on the pro tour too. Still searching for direction, and a reason to turn pro, Arnold wanted most of all to show his father that he was the best amateur golfer in the land.

***

In 1954, at age 24, Palmer was living in Cleveland and working as a sales rep at a paint supply store. Quickly realizing how much he missed a life of full-time golf, he began to work on his game in preparation for the 54th U.S. Amateur, to be played at the Country Club of Detroit. Arnold had never seen the layout of the 6,875-yard course recently refurbished by renowned architect Robert Trent Jones. So upon arriving in Grosse Point, Michigan, he went straight to the country club to become familiar with the great old course. When reporters asked Gene Littler, the 1953 U.S. Amateur titleholder, to identify the golfer who was as slender as a wire and strong as a cable, the one cracking balls on the practice tee, Littler said: "That's Arnold Palmer. He's going to be a great player someday. When he hits the ball, the earth shakes."

In the early rounds of the U.S. Amateur, Palmer won a series of tense, nail-biting matches. In the fifth round he defeated Frank Stranahan, a two-time British Amateur winner and heir to the Champion spark plug fortune. In the quarterfinal he came from behind to beat Don Cherry, the 1953 Canadian Amateur champ. When news reached Latrobe that Arnold had made the semifinals, Deacon and Doris Palmer drove eight hours through the night to Detroit, to be there for the match against Ed Meister, a publishing executive from Cleveland whom Arnold had beaten to win the 1953 Ohio Amateur.

Palmer suffered from a lackluster start. He had played six grueling matches in the previous four days. Match play all the way. Arnold took a 1-up advantage after the morning round of 18 but shot a sloppy 76. Perhaps fatigue was setting in. His game came apart on the first nine of the afternoon, shooting a 39 mostly out of bunkers on the par-70 course. Then, as if cattle-prodded, Palmer's putter suddenly came alive over the final nine, and with adrenaline pumping, he pulled even through 30 holes. On the 36th hole, with the match still square, Arnold hit a miraculous

recovery shot from behind the green that stopped five feet from the cup. Now the pressure was on. He stood for a long time over his knee-knocking putt that would either eliminate him or take the match to extra holes.

"I waited until I was sure I would make it," he said.

It wasn't until the 39th hole—the 510-yard, par-5 3rd hole—that Arnold finally ended the match by hitting a 300-yard drive and a 3-iron second shot onto the green 30 feet from the hole. Meister pushed his tee shot into the trees and struggled to reach the green. After leaving his fourth shot short, Meister took off his cap, extended his hand, and conceded what turned out to be the longest semifinal match in U.S. Amateur history at that time.

Palmer's storybook march into the finals set up the deciding match against a 43-year-old career amateur named Robert Sweeny, scion of a wealthy investment banking family. Sweeny had attended Oxford University, where he met Ian Fleming and was rumored to have been the inspiration for Fleming's most famous character, James Bond, British Secret Service agent 007. A World War II hero, Sweeny helped organize the Eagle Squadron, a group of American pilots who flew for the Royal Air Force, and earned a Distinguished Flying Cross after leading a successful mission against enemy submarines in 1943.

On August 28, 1954, the week before his 25th birthday, Palmer faced the golfing challenge of his life. The Amateur final would pit the groundskeeper's son, who had attended Wake Forest and was seven months out of the Coast Guard, against the socialite who kept tony addresses in London, New York, and Palm Beach.

Palmer sinks a five-foot birdie putt on the 39th hole to defeat Ed Meister, right, in their semifinal match of the U.S. Amateur in Detroit on August 27, 1954. (AP Photo/Preston Stroup)

"We hailed from different galaxies," Palmer noted.

Their head-to-head match was a battle of opposites. According to *Sports Illustrated*, Sweeny was a "graying millionaire playboy who is a celebrity on two continents" and Arnold was a "tanned muscular salesman from Cleveland who literally grew up on a golf course."

Sweeny had won the British Amateur in 1937 and was making his sixth attempt to win the American title. The debonair Londoner embodied the archetypal British aristocrat. A member of ultra-exclusive, posh golf clubs in Florida, London, and France, he was "a dues-paying member of places that would make Latrobe Country Club seem as prestigious as a waffle house," wrote Ian O'Connor in *Arnie & Jack*.

Golf writer Herbert Warren Wind called it a "battle of the classes," and indeed it was. The blue-blooded Sweeny dressed the part as the picture of privilege, wearing a crisp white Lacoste polo shirt and perfectly pressed white linen pants. Palmer, by contrast, looked like a vagabond, with shirt untucked from droopy pants and hair flopping in his eyes every time he swung. Arnold was the underdog, for sure, and the crowd was pulling for him. But he gave the spectators nothing to cheer about in the early going. Sweeny jumped ahead with three birdies over the first four holes. Arnold, outclassed, didn't know what had hit him. He was ashamed that his parents had come all the way from Latrobe to see him play in a daze.

Then Sweeny made a crucial mistake in judgment. As the two men left the 5th tee Sweeny cavalierly put his arm around Arnold's shoulder and haughtily remarked, "I can't go on like this forever." Sweeny's arrogance was a wake-up call and served as the rallying cry for Arnold to make a charge. After being two down through 18 holes, he slugged his way to a 1-up victory on the 36th hole. Striking a blow for the common man, the match ended when Arnold's drive found the fairway while Sweeny's skipped into thick rough. After a failed search for the ball, Sweeny said, "Congratulations, Arnie, you win."

"What other people find in poetry, I find in the flight of a good drive." —Arnold Palmer

---

When Sweeny conceded the match, the tournament director signaled a brass band on the clubhouse terrace, and the band launched into "Hail to the Chief." Arnold hugged his crying mother, Doris, and posed with the Havemeyer Trophy for celebratory photos with his parents. Deacon Palmer, not one to lavish praise, told Arnold, "You did pretty good, boy." Arnold's heart swelled nearly to the breaking point. He'd finally showed his father that he was the best amateur golfer in America. "That victory was the turning point in my life," he said. "It gave me confidence I could compete at the highest level of the game."

***

Arnold Palmer's victory at the U.S. Amateur—he always considered it his eighth major—set in motion a chain of events that would dramatically alter his life forever. Instead of returning to selling paint, Arnold accepted an invitation to play the next week in the Waite Memorial Tournament in Shawnee-on-Delaware, Pennsylvania, which began over Labor Day weekend. It was there that he met the woman who would become his wife for 45 years until her death in 1999. When Arnie arrived, he checked into the Shawnee Inn and almost immediately saw a pretty, dark-haired girl coming down the stairway that led to the main lobby. Arnold fell smitten with 19-year-old Winifred Walzer of Bethlehem,

Arnold Palmer, 24, displays the smile of a champion after defeating Bob Sweeny to win the U.S. Amateur championship in Detroit on August 28, 1954. (AP Photo)

Pennsylvania. She was studying interior design at Brown University's affiliated design school at Pembroke College.

"She had smoky good looks, and her demeanor had a clear sheen of class," Palmer wrote in his autobiography, *A Golfer's Life*. He introduced himself and asked her to come out and watch the golf. The two were inseparable for the rest of the week. Arnold was leading the tournament, but Winnie was on his mind. At the final presentation dinner, he asked her to get married. A tournament official surprised everyone by announcing that Arnold wasn't taking only the tournament trophy home from Shawnee-on-Delaware, but a fiancée, as well. It was a whirlwind courtship, to say the least. "I met him on Tuesday. He asked me to marry him on Saturday," Winnie said.

The couple became engaged and talked about a spring wedding and a honeymoon in England after the 1955 Walker Cup, in which Arnold was set to play at St. Andrews, Scotland. But Arnold grew impatient and plans changed. Shortly before Christmas, Arnold and Winnie decided to get married. Thinking it would be impractical for a married man to remain an amateur, Arnold announced his intention to turn professional, and on November 17, 1954, he signed a contract with Wilson Sporting Goods Company. He and Winnie recited their vows on December 20, 1954, in Falls Church, Virginia, near the home of Arnold's sister, Cheech. Winnie's parents stayed away because her father never liked the idea of Winnie marrying a future struggling pro, who he doubted could properly provide for his daughter. With borrowed money to stake them, the happy couple set off to honeymoon on the PGA Tour circuit.

In Palmer's rookie year on the PGA Tour, he and his new wife traveled to tournaments with a dusty and dilapidated trailer hitched to his secondhand 1952 coral-pink Ford. From his hometown in Latrobe, Pennsylvania, they drove to Minnesota, Milwaukee, Toledo, Chicago, and Detroit like a couple of golfing gypsies. At Meadowbrook Country Club outside Detroit, Arnold was driving practice balls while veteran pros George Fazio and Toney Penna watched.

Arnold overheard Fazio say, "That's the kid Arnold Palmer. He just won the National Amateur."

Penna replied, "Well, better tell him to get a job. With that swing of his, he'll *never* make it out here."

The comment chafed Arnold. He wasn't perfect and neither was his swing. If his swing was not textbook, it was ferocious. He did not so much hit a golf ball as attack it. He seemed to heave all 185 pounds of his chiseled five-foot-ten body at the ball. But Arnold believed in himself—and his makeshift swing. He was confident that positive results would soon convert his critics. Indeed, in 1968, after Arnold won the Bob Hope Classic for the third time, Penna winked and said, "Palmer, you're beginning to swing that club pretty good."

"I watched this guy, he looked like Popeye hitting these drilling 9-irons that were going about 12 feet high. I said, you know, look at this guy, man, this guy's strong. Boy, can he hit. He'd really drill it." —Jack Nicklaus

---

Arnold Palmer desperately wanted to make it on the PGA Tour, and he desperately wanted to quiet the naysayers. In April 1955, at his first Masters, he tied for

Palmer tees off during the St. Paul Open at Keller Golf Course in St. Paul, Minnesota, on July 9, 1955, one month before winning his first pro tournament. (AP Photo)

10th place, good for $696. His winnings were enough to buy a new trailer, which he and Winnie drove all the way across the United States to San Francisco for the U.S. Open, then to Portland and on to Vancouver. Winnie was devoted to her husband. To Winnie, he was Arn. For years she was wife and secretary and business consultant. She handled the family finances. She balanced the books, paid the bills, made the travel arrangements, mailed the entry blanks, and devoted her entire attention to one goal: making sure that her husband's mind was free to concentrate on his golf game.

The newlyweds lived life on a shoestring. In late August 1955, Winnie and Arnold Palmer arrived at Weston Golf and Country Club, along the banks of the Humber River on the outskirts of Toronto, for the Canadian Open. To save money, they camped in a field behind the course superintendent's shed. The relatively unknown rookie started turning heads, though, by shooting a blistering 64 in the opening round for eight-under par. A second-round 67 and then another 64 followed. Palmer showed glimpses of the aggressive playing style and personality that would endear him to millions of golf fans in the decades to come. He confidently sank 20-foot putts that would have traveled 40 feet if the backside of the cups hadn't swallowed them. By the fourth round, Toronto golf fans had adopted Palmer as their own, with a gallery of spectators 6,000 strong following the rookie golfer from hole to hole, lining the fairways and encircling the green.

"I don't think that I could've had any more rooters if I had been playing in my hometown," Palmer said of the supportive fans after the tournament. The spectators foreshadowed the immense crowds, nicknamed "Arnie's Army," that would trail him at competitions in the years to come. Beyond the cheers of encouragement, the Toronto spectators helped Arnold in another way. Three times his shots went careening off course, and three times the ball struck an onlooker and rolled back into play. In the third round, on the 7th hole, Arnold swung his 4-wood and launched the ball straight over the green and into the crowd. The ball struck one spectator square in the forehead, then caromed back onto the green. "[The] chap, with a dent right between his eyes from a Palmer shot, brushed the injury aside," said an onlooker quoted by James A. Barclay in *Golf in Canada: A History*, "and utilized the occasion to request Palmer's autograph when the latter rushed up to enquire on his condition."

Palmer held a commanding six-stroke lead going into the final round. There he gave Canadian fans a glimpse of the future, eschewing caution and going for broke. He snap-hooked his drive into the woods on the 6th hole and found his ball lying near an old fallen tree. Rather than try to protect the lead by chipping out, Arnold saw a small gap through the trees and was contemplating taking that incredibly difficult shot when his playing partner, Tommy Bolt, bellowed: "For God's sake, Arnie. Chip it out into the fairway. You've got a six-stroke lead!"

Palmer was determined to follow his instincts. He reached into his bag, took out a 6-iron, and ripped a clean shot through the small gap in the trees onto the green, salvaging a double-bogey on the hole. The gallery let loose a tremendous cheer. Such aggressive play—spurning safe, conservative shots for high-risk, high-reward gambles—would become Palmer's trademark on the course and was central to his appeal to his millions of fans over the duration of his career. Arnold later said that caution might be appropriate for some things, but not for golf.

"That was my way," he said. "My father taught me to go get it. If you're shooting between two trees with a 10-foot opening, and you try to calculate the percentages, you'd be there forever."

Never one to tarry, Arnold solidified his lead. Thousands of spectators who were crowded around the 18th green erupted into a thunderous cheer as he sank his putt for par, finishing the day with a 70 and a total, four-round score of 265—23 under par and two off the Canadian Open record. Arnold picked up his ball, kissed it, and threw it into the crowd. Then he embraced his wife, Winnie, who pointed out that it was one year to the day that Arnold had captured the National Amateur Championship. Arnold earned $2,400 for winning his first professional tournament. Jack Burke Jr., the runner-up and eventual 1956 Masters and PGA Championship winner, proved prescient with his post-tournament statement to the press.

"I think you'll be hearing a lot about Arnold from here in," he said.

After the festivities, Arnold and Winnie set off for a brief holiday at a fishing retreat in Ontario before heading to the next tournament stop in Montreal. He was the new Canadian Open champion. He'd won his first PGA tournament. He sat at the end of the dock fishing and drinking cold beers as the sun set over the horizon. He was happy and at peace.

Palmer completed his first season as a professional golfer with one win and $7,958 in official prize money. By Christmas, a pregnant Winnie was well along with their first child, and the couple talked about buying a piece of land near Latrobe Country Club. Living out of a suitcase, they agreed, was no way to raise a baby, and they really needed a home of their own.

The Palmers purchased a three-acre lot on the property where so many years before he and his Pap used to hunt pheasant and quail. Arnold and Winnie built a ranch house overlooking Latrobe Country Club. Peggy was born in February 1956, and the couple had another daughter, Amy, two years later. Winnie stayed home to care for the children and help Arnold with finances and other business

A license plate signed by the Keystone State's famous hero. (Authors' Collection)

matters. Arnold took advantage of his favorite hobby, fly-ing, to sky-hop between tournaments and visit his growing family. The Latrobe Airport was only about a mile from his home. Arnold looked forward to one day buying and piloting his own plane.

***

Though he had turned pro rather late in life due to his tour of duty with the Coast Guard, Arnold Palmer was quickly making up ground. The Canadian Open victory in 1955 served as a launching pad for his career. Palmer won two more titles in 1956, and four more in '57, before his major breakthrough at the 1958 Masters. Arnold arrived at National Golf Club in Augusta, Georgia, having won the eighth title of his career at the St. Petersburg Open, but had very little professional major championship experience. He had yet to play in a British Open or PGA Championship and had finished tied for seventh a year earlier at the Masters. Palmer, a rising star, and Ben Hogan, a fading legend, played a practice round together, and afterward, Hogan broke standard practice by eating lunch at a different table rather than with Palmer. That peeved Arnold, but not as much as overhearing Hogan wonder aloud, "How did Palmer get an invitation to the Masters?" A chilly relationship developed between these two golfing giants that would never thaw.

The 1958 Masters tournament proved eventful for many reasons. Two bridges across Rae's Creek were dedicated in honor of Ben Hogan and Byron Nelson. It was also the year *Sports Illustrated* golf writer Herbert Warren Wind came up with the term Amen Corner to describe the famous stretch of holes—Nos. 11, 12, and 13—where Rae's Creek intersects the course. These three holes have played a vital role in determining many a Masters winner—and loser. On this occasion, it was a rules dispute on the 12th hole during the final round that is still much debated after all these years.

It was the first year that soldiers from nearby Camp Gordon were offered free admission and were recruited to run the scoreboards at Augusta National. Over the first three rounds, Palmer, a Coast Guard veteran, played his way into a tie for first with Sam Snead. Arnold won over the troops and most of the rest of the crowd. By the time he teed off with Ken Venturi on Sunday morning, Arnie's Army was officially born, and its enthusiasm helped carry Palmer to new heights.

That's not to imply it was all smooth sailing for Arnold. When he reached the 12th hole, the famed 155-yard par-3, Arnold was one shot ahead of Venturi for the overall lead. There had been a lot of rain in the previous days. Palmer's tee shot landed behind the green and plugged in a bank about a foot from the bunker. Arnold believed he was entitled to relief because the ball was embedded. He asked for a free drop, but rules officials on the scene turned him down, requiring Arnold to play the ball as it lay. There was an animated argument. Eventually, he played the embedded ball and scraped it out of the turf, hitting a poor chip shot past the hole, then two-putting for a double-bogey 5. Venturi made par and assumed the lead. Believing he was entitled to relief and that rules officials eventually would agree, Arnold announced he was playing a second ball. He returned to the spot where the ball had been, took a drop, and made par.

Venturi always thought Arnold played the second ball incorrectly.

"I firmly believe that [Palmer] did wrong, and that he knows that I know he did wrong," Venturi wrote in his 2004 autobiography *Getting Up & Down: My 60 Years in Golf.* "That is why, to this day, it has left me with an uncomfortable feeling."

Arnold disagreed.

"There was never a question in my mind that I wasn't right about the 12th hole," he wrote in *Playing By the Rules.* "I was very confident that I was right and I played with that confidence."

Arnold invoked Rule 3-3a, which states that when there is doubt as to how to proceed, the golfer can drop a second ball and complete the hole with two golf balls. Before turning in his scorecard, the golfer reports the situation to the committee, which issues a ruling, and then everyone knows which ball (and, therefore, which score) is counted. So Palmer made a double-bogey with the original, embedded ball, then dropped a second ball and made a par. Which score counted? Was Arnold leading by one, or Venturi leading by one?

The question was still unresolved at the 13th hole when Palmer played the shot that, in retrospect, won him the tournament. After both players had driven the same length from the tee box, Venturi deliberately played safe and hit his second shot short, setting up an easy pitching wedge and a birdie putt. Arnold, displaying the boldness that characterized him in his prime, went for the green with his second shot, cracking a 3-wood that carried the creek. The ball landed hole-high, and Arnold made the 18-foot putt for eagle to propel him into the lead.

Palmer signed this 1958 Masters clubhouse badge belonging to Bobby Jones's secretary, Jean Marshall, after winning his first green jacket. He always made sure his autograph was legible. (Heritage Auctions)

Providence arrived at the next hole. Arnold's boyhood hero, Bobby Jones, codesigner of the Augusta National course and founder of the Masters, informed Arnold that he had indeed been entitled to relief at the 12th hole and that his par-3 score would count instead of the double-bogey 5. Palmer wound up winning by a shot over Fred Hawkins and Doug Ford, the 1957 Masters champion, and by two over Venturi. The two-stroke swing at the 12th hole turned out to be a huge difference maker. At age 28, Arnold won his first Masters. At the time, he was Augusta's youngest champion.

"[Winning the 1958 Masters] told me something that I needed to know about myself. That with the right kind of focus and hard work and maybe a little bit of luck, I could be the best player in the game." —Arnold Palmer

---

"Arnold Palmer was born April 6, 1958, on the back nine of Augusta National Golf Club," *Sports Illustrated* would later reflect.

Palmer entered the national sporting consciousness by winning his first green jacket at Augusta just as television was becoming a burgeoning industry. His timing was impeccable. This was just the third year of broadcast coverage for the Masters, with only the 15th through 18th holes shown. Arnold and the television cameras formed a powerful pair.

Sam Snead and Palmer rehash their scores after third-round play at the Masters, on April 5, 1958. Snead and Palmer wound up in a tie for the lead with a 54-hole total of 211. (AP Photo)

"Television and Palmer took over golf simultaneously," Jim Murray, the *Los Angeles Times*'s Pulitzer Prize-winning sports columnist, once wrote.

The camera loved Arnold's blond, rugged good looks. He played raw golf, with rough edges, yet he oozed integrity. Television viewers took to Arnold's easy charm and fearless style. Controlled emotions also bolstered Arnold's charisma. Yes, his facial expressions could be extreme, but he seemed always in control, the model of confidence, always going for his shot. At a time when television was first coming into our homes, Arnie came into our living rooms with approachability and a grittiness that made us want to watch golf. It made us want to play golf too.

Ben Hogan was a superb player, but he didn't make golf popular. Hogan's personality was as cuddly as a porcupine. Palmer was something else. He was a new golf superstar with mass appeal. Arnold captured the public imagination in a way no golfer had before. His telegenic personality and magnetic appeal was different from an upper-crust game played at exclusive country clubs; his was enjoyed by suburban hackers and average Joes. Arnold played golf like the guy next door—if the guy next door was hugely talented, that is.

"Palmer went to bed at night with charisma, and he woke up the next morning with more." —Sam Snead

In the America of 1958, the war-hero president, Dwight D. Eisenhower, loved golf and conducted the nation's

Palmer groans as his putt rolls past the hole on 18 during the final round of the Masters on April 6, 1959. Palmer was tied for the 54-hole lead but faltered to a 74 and a 286 total, finishing two strokes behind winner Art Wall Jr. (AP Photo/Horace Cort)

business on the course. A postwar economic expansion led to an emerging middle class, a migration to the suburbs, and an increase in leisure time. Into that mix of conditions came a bolt of lightning named Arnold Palmer that made golf the coolest sport on the planet—and Arnold its coolest competitor. President Eisenhower had asked Augusta National Golf Club Chairman Clifford Roberts to arrange a friendly game with the winner of the Masters, and as luck would have it, that champion would be Arnold Palmer. Again, perfect timing. Arnold and Ike became lifelong friends.

Arnold's love affair with the Masters would last a half century. He won the event four times—1958, 1960, 1962, and 1964—and played in 50 consecutive Masters before taking final bows in 2004. Following his 1958 Masters victory, Arnold went on to win the St. Petersburg Open and the Pepsi Open and finished up the year No. 1 on the PGA Tour money list with more than $40,000 in prize money. He was beginning to become a household name and blaze a path to greatness that foreshadowed his immense impact on the pro game.

CHAPTER 3

FOUR YEARS OF GLORY

Arnold Palmer got off to a fast start on the PGA Tour in 1960. By mid-March he had won tournaments in four states and on both coasts: in Palm Springs, San Antonio, Baton Rouge, and Pensacola. He passed up the Azalea Open at Wilmington, North Carolina, in order to arrive at Augusta National a week in advance. He

Palmer escapes trouble during the 1962 Masters. His caddie, Nathaniel Avery, didn't like wearing No. 13, but Arnold wasn't superstitious. (AP Photo)

checked in at the registration desk and asked to be enrolled as number 13, because this was his 13th tournament of the year. His caddie, Nathaniel Avery, better known as "Iron Man," had to wear a big 13 like a target on his back all week. Avery didn't like it, but Arnold was not the superstitious sort. He was now 30 years old. In less than four years as a pro, he had won 13 PGA Tour events, including the 1958 Masters, and then quickly added four more wins to bring his ledger up to 17 in the run-up to the 1960 Masters.

Palmer often played his best in the big tournaments. For one thing, his game was better adapted to the tougher courses. For another, he got more keyed up when an important title was at stake. Arnold thrived on competition, the more formidable the better. And he enjoyed taming the most difficult of layouts. "When I get on a hard, exacting course, I feel as if I'm wrestling a bear," he told the *Saturday Evening Post* in 1960.

Such a course is Augusta National. It's a course that will shatter your confidence—even break you—when you least expect it. The Masters may have been Arnold Palmer's favorite tournament, but it wasn't always kind to him. Palmer won there in 1958 and then kicked away the 1959 tournament. He blew the lead on the back nine on the final day. Palmer had a three-shot lead when his 6-iron found the water at the par-3 12th, leading to a triple-bogey 6. Palmer bravely bounced back with birdies on 13 and 15, but then he missed an easy three-footer for par and bogeyed 17. All the while, Art Wall Jr., a fellow Pennsylvanian from the Poconos, birdied five of the last six holes to beat Arnold by two strokes.

Wall put on a dazzling display of finishing golf, but afterward the newspaper headlines emphasized Palmer losing rather than Wall winning. That's what happens when the defending Masters champion blows a big one. Said Palmer, "If I had made a par on 12, I probably would have won the tournament by six shots."

Because of that 1959 disappointment, Arnold went to the Masters in 1960 more determined than ever.

***

Palmer teed off at Augusta in 1960 as the crowd favorite. In the first round, he shot a five-under-par 67, with an 18-foot putt on the final hole, and led by two strokes. He putted poorly the next day for a 73 but stayed ahead by a stroke. Keeping the pedal to the medal, he shot a third-round 72. That sent Arnold into the last round with a one-stroke edge over five tough cookies—Ben Hogan, Ken Venturi, Dow Finsterwald, Billy Casper, and Julius Boros.

The final round quickly developed into a two-way battle between Venturi and Palmer. Venturi said he played the final round without once looking at the scoreboard or checking on what his opponent was doing. With Arnold it was just the opposite. He got reports at every hole. Palmer was on the 14th when Venturi finished with a solid 70 for a score of 283. It appeared the victory would go to Venturi, who was sitting in Butler Cabin with a one-stroke lead.

Golfers like to say it's best to be in the clubhouse with a good score, as Venturi was, and make the guys on the course come and get you. Palmer knew precisely what he

Palmer, left, accepts congratulations from Billy Casper on the occasion of his second Masters championship, in 1960. Palmer carded birdies on the last two holes to nip Ken Venturi by a stroke. (AP Photo/Horace Cort)

had to do. It wouldn't be easy. He needed to play the last two holes in one-under par to tie, and two-under to win.

"I was confident I could get at least one birdie on the final two holes to tie him," said Palmer. "Somehow, I always feel I can get a birdie when I need it."

On 17, a par-4 at 400 yards downwind, Arnold hit a good drive, then played an 8-iron pitch that left him about 27 feet below the cup. Twice he walked away from the putt, distracted by spectators behind the green who were moving back and forth, directly in his line. Over the ball a third time, he tapped it firmly. The ball hesitated at the lip of the cup and then toppled in. As it disappeared, Palmer leaped into the air. He got his first birdie and tied Venturi. Half the job was done. There was high tension and wild excitement all around Palmer at the 18th tee.

"The only sensation I felt was that my mouth was awfully dry," he said later. "I would have given 10 bucks for a sip of water."

On 18, a par-4 at 420 yards uphill, Palmer's first concern was to make sure of par and stay in a tie with Venturi. Arnold kept his drive on the straightaway and punched a 6-iron approach shot that landed five feet to the left of the flagstick. He studied the putt for birdie very carefully. He asked the newsreel men to stop their cameras. Once Arnold was sure of the break of the green, he did not fuss much over the putt. His ball rolled toward the cup. It dropped. That was the tournament. It took Arnold a moment to realize that it was all over, all won. He retrieved his ball and walked a normal stride or two when he suddenly started jumping all over the place and dancing a zany little jig. Arnie was

exuberant. It was the sort of finish that led the legendary Bobby Jones to say, "If I ever had to have one putt to win a title for me, I'd rather have Arnold Palmer hit it for me than anybody I ever saw."

Palmer lived up to the favorite's role, shocking Ken Venturi and thrilling a huge TV audience by birdie-ing the final two holes at Augusta National to win by a

Palmer signs his winning Masters scorecard in 1960. He shot a 70 for a four-round total of 282. (AP Photo)

stroke. Palmer was just the second wire-to-wire winner at the Masters, following Craig Wood in 1941. This was Arnold's second Masters championship and also the second major of his career. Most of all, it was a stunning display of steely nerves. Bobby Jones called it one of the most dramatic victories he had ever seen, and the legendary amateur's words generated plenty of international buzz. But the buzz was almost ordinary compared to what happened in June at the U.S. Open.

**

The 1960 United States Open was played at Cherry Hills Country Club outside Denver. It was there that Palmer mounted the greatest final-round charge in U.S. Open history, overcoming a seven-stroke deficit and passing the 14 golfers ahead of him. Palmer jumped over everyone, just as he had predicted. It was an unlikely come-from-behind triumph. Also unlikely was the way Palmer captured the national imagination by guaranteeing the win, much like Babe Ruth calling his shot in the 1932 World Series. The rest is history. He staged what became his trademark "charge" on the last day, and his six-under 65 earned him the victory by two strokes over a pudgy, 20-year-old amateur named Jack Nicklaus.

A famous photograph shows Arnie's jubilation as he tosses his visor into the air after sinking the clinching putt. As the visor was spinning, the Palmer legend was born. It was an even more fantastic finish than his one-shot triumph at the Masters and one that forever etched Arnold Palmer into the minds of the American sporting consciousness.

Just as Arnold burst onto the scene and began to collect dramatic victories, America's fascination with television was exploding. Television sets, which numbered only 3.8 million in 1950, were in almost 46 million American homes by 1960.

"Arnold meant everything to golf. Are you kidding me? I mean, without his charisma, without his personality in conjunction with TV—it was just the perfect symbiotic growth. You finally had someone who had this charisma, and they're capturing it on TV for the very first time. Everyone got hooked to the game of golf via TV because of Arnold." —Tiger Woods

---

"The camera is strange," Frank Chirkinian, the longtime CBS golf producer who worked his first Masters in 1959, once told *Golf Digest*. "It's all revealing. It either loves you or hates you, and it loved Arnold."

He leaped off the small black-and-white screen with a winning smile, easygoing manner, and rugged athleticism. Palmer's aggressive risk/reward approach to golf made him the ideal leading man for the hot new medium. He didn't lay up or leave putts short. His go-for-broke style made for compelling theater. He hit the ball with authority and for distance and ushered in an aggressive, in-your-face power game, rarely seen in the often stoic and staid sport. "In a

Arnie displays the winning smile and rugged athleticism that made him a crossover star. (AP Photo/Dozier Mobley)

sports world. It was how he played. He did not so much navigate a course as attack it. Going for those big drives meant he played out of the woods and ditches with equal abandon, resulting in a string of memorable charges. And if he did not win, he at least lost with flair. Audiences viewed Arnold as must-see TV. Golf's television ratings soared. He was taking the game to the masses. Quite simply, he made golf cool.

"I used to hear cheers go up from the crowd around Palmer," Lee Trevino said. "And I never knew whether he'd made a birdie or just hitched up his pants."

***

Having won both the Masters and the U.S. Open in 1960, Palmer yearned to add the British Open and the PGA Championship to his repertoire, or a modern Grand Slam. As a boy, Arnie read books about Bobby Jones, who as an amateur in 1930 swept the United States Amateur and Open Championships and the British Amateur and Open Championships all in a single year. He dreamed of someday duplicating the feat of his idol. He started thinking about the idea of a pro Grand Slam—winning the Masters, the U.S. Open, the British Open, and the PGA (Professional Golfers Association of America) Championship. Ben Hogan won the first three of these in his great year of 1953 but had to pass up the PGA. No golfer ever has taken all four in the same year. Yet Arnold felt confident that, with a little luck, he could be the man to do it.

In July, he made the pilgrimage to Scotland's St. Andrews links with hopes of winning the third leg. St.

sport that was high society," broadcaster Vin Scully said, "he made it *High Noon.*"

No one did more to popularize the sport than Palmer. His dashing presence singlehandedly took golf out of the country clubs and into the mainstream. But it was more than his scoring and shot making that captivated the

On the 18th green, Palmer is a tap-in away from a final-round 66 to win his first Los Angeles Open title, on January 8, 1963. (AP Photo)

Andrews is an ancient course dating back to the 1500s. Some call it the birthplace of the game. After the first two rounds on the Old Course, Palmer was tied for third and trailed the leader by seven strokes. Only four back starting the last round, he mounted a late charge with birdies on 17 and 18. The reserved, stiff-upper-lipped British crowd transformed itself into a suddenly raucous gallery, an early version of Arnie's Army from across the pond. It so unnerved the leader, Australia's Kel Nagle, that he two-putted from two feet on 18, but his par nevertheless gave him a one-shot win

Arnold walks with his wife, Winnie, and father, Deacon, at the start of the British Open at St. Andrews, Scotland, on July 7, 1960. Palmer's pilgrimage helped make the British Open important in the United States. (AP Photo)

over Palmer. Arnold's chance at the Grand Slam vanished. To date, the challenge of winning the four major PGA tournaments in a single season remains a Holy Grail for professional golfers, who credit Palmer with the concept.

Palmer became golfing royalty in 1960, his watershed year. He won two majors and eight tournaments overall

and was recognized for making the British Open important again in the United States. Palmer was the leading money winner on the PGA Tour each year from 1960 to 1963, and its Player of the Year in 1960 and 1962. Fittingly, the award for the leading money winner each year is now named for him.

"Palmer on a golf course was Jack Dempsey with his man on the ropes, Henry Aaron with a three-and-two fastball, Rod Laver at set point, Joe Montana with a minute to play, A.J. Foyt with a lap to go and a car to catch." *—Los Angeles Times* **columnist Jim Murray**

Palmer's dominance over the field lasted four years, beginning in 1960, when he ushered in what has been called golf's Golden Era. From 1960 to 1963, he won six major championships and 29 titles, finished second 10 times, and had 66 top 10s on the PGA Tour. He also captained the U.S. team to victory in the Ryder Cup in 1963. It was his greatest stretch of golf. These years should be placed in golf's seminal time capsule, as it represents an age when the ever-expanding power of television intersected with the drawing power of Arnold Palmer.

***

Until Palmer, the British Open was mostly for British golfers. It was Palmer who convinced his colleagues that they could never consider themselves champions unless they had won the Claret Jug. Palmer finished second at the British Open on his first trip in 1960. But he won the British Open in each of the next two years, at Royal Birkdale in England in 1961 and at Royal Troon in Scotland in 1962. His presence there helped salvage the game's oldest championship and elevated the Open back among the game's best tournaments.

"It was a nice championship to place on a list of achievements but not an essential one," the *London Independent* wrote of American indifference to the event. "Palmer, almost single-handedly, changed all that."

The British Open in 1961, played on the links of the Royal Birkdale Golf Club, close by the Irish Sea, near Liverpool, was plagued by miserable weather, which caused devastation to refreshment tents and reduced Royal Birkdale to shambles. Palmer adjusted his game after the wind battered his shots in the early going. He opened on Wednesday with a 70, two off the lead. He often teed off with a 1-iron to keep the ball low and did the same with his other irons. Esteemed British golf writer Henry Longhurst described Palmer's approach shots as "screeching waist-high

Palmer shows the grit and determination Brits found so appealing during the British Open at Royal Birkdale Golf Club, England, on July 13, 1961. (AP Photo)

bullets that somehow retained enough backspin to bite on the soft Birkdale greens."

Gale-force winds at 50 miles an hour tormented the field on the second day. Arnold fired a commendable 73 on Thursday to tie for second, one stroke back. Palmer might have had a 72, were it not for a one-stroke penalty that he called on himself when the wind moved his ball an instant before he struck it. Torrential rains prevented the 36-hole final on Friday. Palmer said of the conditions, "What hadn't blown away before was washed away."

The Royal and Ancient postponed play until Saturday. Longhurst wrote that Palmer was unfazed by the weather.

"If necessary, I'm prepared to play in a rowboat," Palmer declared.

Arnie's good sportsmanship and grit appealed to the Brits. When the rain subsided the next day, Palmer made noise early in the morning with a 32 on the outward nine. His 69 gave him a one-stroke lead over Dai Rees of Wales going into the afternoon round. Palmer enjoyed a four-shot lead at the final turn, but Rees soon rallied to within one. Arnold's title hopes dimmed when his drive on the par-4 15th hole rolled off the fairway. His ball settled in the deep rough, buried beneath some blackberry bushes. Palmer's caddie, as well as interested bystanders, urged him to punch out with a wedge. Instead of surrendering, the swashbuckling Palmer elected to go for the green. He grabbed a 6-iron from his bag and took a mighty rip—sending a huge divot flying—and knocked the ball through the thicket as if it were a scythe. His ball soared onto the narrow putting sur-face some 150 yards away. This feat of strength and skill brought gasps from the gallery.

"I have never hit a ball so hard in my life," said Palmer later.

Former British Open champion Henry Cotton called the thunderous strike out of the rough "one of the greatest shots ever."

Perhaps no other golfer would have dared that shot.

"I saw the opening," Palmer later explained. "I was sure I would make it. Nobody else did."

After making his 4 on the 15th, Palmer parred in and won the Open by one stroke over Rees. The second shot on 15 lives on in the game's mythology. Birkdale has since honored his shot from the rough with a plaque installed on what is now the 16th hole. Thousands of people have seen it and recall Arnold's remarkable feats and inimitable style. While his approach on the course wasn't a model of aesthetics—the whirlybird follow-through, the trademark pigeon-toed putting stance—it sure worked for him.

In his victory speech he thanked everyone, even remembering to recognize Birkdale's greenskeepers. Such instances exemplified the small-town Pennsylvanian's life-long reputation for humility, and the down-to-earth character that made him so popular to legions of fans around the world.

"He has no fancy airs and grace," British golf commentator Henry Longhurst once wrote. "He wears no fancy clothes. He makes no fancy speeches. He simply does and

Arnold and Winnie arrive at New York's Idlewild Airport, from England, on July 16, 1961. Palmer holds the trophy he received for winning the British Open a day earlier. (AP Photo)

says exactly the right thing at the right time, and that is enough."

Palmer captured the hearts and respect of British golf fans with his dramatic Open victory in 1961, the fourth of his seven major titles. He was the first American to win the Claret Jug since Ben Hogan in 1953. At that time, many American players thought it cost-prohibitive to play over-

seas. The top US golfers seldom competed in the United Kingdom; they didn't like to leave the rich American tour for an event that offered a first prize of only about $3,500. But Palmer considered the British Open an essential cog in the modern Grand Slam.

"I'll miss tournaments worth about $100,000, but I don't care," he once said. "I got into this business primarily to win championships."

***

Arnold Palmer was all risky business at the 1962 Masters championship. After 54 holes, he had a two-shot lead over Dow Finsterwald and a four-stroke lead over Gary Player. But Arnie's game disintegrated during the final round. He made three bogeys in the first seven holes, and then double-bogeyed the 10th hole. It was a disastrous start. By the time Palmer reached the 16th hole his collapse seemed inevitable. He was two strokes behind with three holes remaining. But Arnie rallied at the end with birdies on Nos. 16 and 17 to tie Player at eight-under, and Finsterwald bogeyed No. 17 to fall back to eight-under, as well. All three parred No. 18, forcing an unprecedented three-way tie. An 18-hole playoff was staged the following day.

On Sunday, Palmer had shot 75 to Player's 71 and Finsterwald's 73. For the playoff on Monday, Arnold played the first nine holes in woeful fashion to fall three strokes behind Player. The estimated 40,000 spectators saw Arnie hit golf shots that would have sent a weekend warrior scurrying to his pro for help. But Arnold was not going down without a fight. Suddenly, just when he seemed utterly defeated, Palmer birdied the long 10th hole and the diffi-

Palmer at the Masters, on April 9, 1962. He won the three-man playoff against Gary Player, left, and Dow Finsterwald. (AP Images)

cult par-3 12th. He smashed a daring shot to the green and two-putted for a birdie on the treacherous 13th and then sank a 16-footer to birdie the 14th. Two more birdies on 15 and 16 completed the spectacular stretch of six birdies in nine holes.

Galleries call it "charging," and it's a word they reserve just for Palmer. In five holes he went from three strokes down to four up. He finished with 68. Player posted a respectable 71 but was no match for Palmer's strong finish. No one should have been surprised by Palmer's back-nine charge. He played the final nine in 17-under for the tournament. Palmer's caddie, Nathaniel "Iron Man" Avery, could see the charge coming.

"He just jerks at his glove, tugs at his trouser belt, and starts walking fast," he said after the round. "When Mr. Arnold does that, everybody better watch out. He's going to stampede anything in his way."

It was the first three-man playoff in tournament history. Player had been trying to become the tournament's first back-to-back champion, and Palmer's victory gave him a measure of revenge against his South African rival. Arnold Palmer didn't often lose on the final hole. But at the 1961 Masters, he had done just that when he made a double bogey on 18, giving Player the win. A year later, Palmer and Player were at it again. The 1962 Masters was the golf duel of the year. This time, the indomitable Arnold Palmer, performing his high-wire act that electrifies his galleries, slipped on the green jacket for the third time in five years.

***

Arnold Palmer's second major championship of 1962, and sixth of his career, was a runaway at the British Open at Troon Golf Club in Scotland. Old Troon is a bleak and gloomy links course situated by the Firth of Clyde on the western coast of Scotland. The fairways are narrow, splotched with steep-sided bunkers that look like moon craters. It is one of those eerie British courses that can unhinge a mentally fragile duffer. *Sports Illustrated* described Troon as being "surrounded by evil dunes, vile shrubs and an atmosphere more suited to the Hound of the Baskervilles than to sport."

When Palmer made his British Open championship debut in 1960, Kel Nagle spoiled it for him, beating Arnie by a stroke for the title. At the 1962 British Open, it was Palmer who finished first and Nagle who wound up second—but it wasn't close. Palmer finished at 12 under par, six shots ahead of runner-up Nagle—and at least 13 strokes better than anyone else in the field. How dominant was Arnie? There were only five rounds in the 60s the entire tournament, and Palmer had three of them. He finished 69-67-69.

***

"I have a tip that can take five strokes off anyone's golf game: it's called an eraser." —Arnold Palmer

***

Palmer called his mauling of Scotland's fiercely strange Troon course the best four rounds of his career. He never once held back from his attacking style, not even at the dangerous

One month after winning his third Masters title, Arnold spends time with Winnie and daughters Amy, left, and Peggy, at their Latrobe home. (AP Photo)

par-5 11th hole with the railway line running just a few yards to the right side of the green. The third round was the great separator, when Arnie ran away from the field. It all happened so fast, like a ninja assassin. From a deep bunker alongside the 12th green, he got up and down in two shots to save par, thrusting his arms in the air with joy after sinking the putt from eight feet. Jump-started, he then birdied No. 13 with a six-foot putt, parred 14, birdied 15 and 16, and birdied the par-3 17th with a 25-footer—four dazzling birdies in five holes! He finished in 67, breaking the course record by two strokes and taking control of the British Open, as well.

Palmer was just the second golfer (after Ben Hogan in 1953) to win The Masters and the British Open in the same year. And his 276 total lowered the tournament scoring record by two shots and stood until 1977. His furious comebacks and breathless triumphs turned the Yank from Latrobe into an American cousin. He was the favorite among the stiffening-ly proper British golfing public. Fans admired his personal charm, praised his reverence for golf's classic traditions, and marveled at his daring play.

While Brits were accustomed to homegrown poker-faced sports heroes, Palmer's face was genuinely expressive. He would stride down a fairway acknowledging his army of fans with a sunny smile and a raised club, "like Sir Lancelot amid the multitude in Camelot," Ira Berkow wrote in the *New York Times*.

And the television cameras followed along. Back home in America, the *Times* stated, Palmer almost "single-handedly stimulated TV coverage of golf, widening the game's popularity among a postwar generation of World War II veterans enjoying economic boom times and a sprawling green suburbia."

Palmer's back-to-back achievement at Royal Birkdale and Royal Troon made it cool for Americans to go to the British Open again. After Palmer, they all came.

"When Palmer went," said former U.S. Golf Association Executive Director Frank Hannigan, "all the other Americans went, too, and the British Open was restored to its former majesty."

Along with Arnie came the riches of bigger purses for everyone. Prize money on the PGA Tour increased from $820,360 in 1957 to $3,704,445 in 1966. As the world's best players journeyed to compete on the Open links, prize money increased there too. Nick Faldo, during Palmer's farewell at St. Andrews in 1995, may have put it best when he said, "If Arnold hadn't come here in 1960 we'd probably all be in a shed on the beach."

Mark O'Meara went a step further.

"He made it possible for all of us to make a living in this game."

***

As legendary and dramatic as Palmer's victories were, so, too, were his losses in major championships. Arnie's setbacks were epic. At the Masters in 1959, he blew a lead on the back nine and lost to Art Wall Jr. Two years later, he needed only a par 4 on the final hole to become the first golfer to win at Augusta National in consecutive years. But after a good drive—and after accepting premature congratulations from a friend he knew in the gallery—Arnold skidded his 7-iron approach into a bunker, blasted out over

Palmer, hoping to bag another U.S. Open title, arrives for a practice round at Oakmont in 1962. The trophy was decided in a playoff between Palmer and Jack Nicklaus. (AP Images/Paul Vathis)

A fan needed just $16 for a ticket to the 18-hole U.S. Open playoff between Arnold Palmer and Jack Nicklaus at Oakmont Country Club on June 17, 1962. (Heritage Auctions)

the green, chipped 15 feet past the cup, and two-putted for a double-bogey 6 to lose by a stroke to Gary Player.

It was all part of being Arnold Palmer, once described by the writer Alfred Wright as "that cataclysm with legs." Palmer lost playoffs in the U.S. Open in 1962 to Jack Nicklaus at Oakmont, near Pittsburgh, and in 1963 to

Julius Boros at the Country Club in Brookline, Massachusetts. When Nicklaus beat Palmer in the 1962 U.S. Open playoff—it was Nicklaus's first major victory—it may have signaled a changing of the guard. It also marked the beginning of a great rivalry.

"At times we became so hyper about beating each other that we let someone else go right by us and win," Palmer said. "But our competition was fun and good for the game."

Win or lose, Palmer was often at his best in the big tournaments. For one thing, he could adapt his game to the different golf courses. For another, he got more keyed up when an important title was at stake. Arnold thrived on competition, the more formidable the better. His career trajectory was healthy and strong. Maybe he could play golf forever. His father insisted that Arnold could play competitively until he was 50, at least.

"The main thing is to take care of yourself, boy," Pap told his son. "A man's body is like a tractor. Keep it in shape, and it will be serviceable for years."

CHAPTER 4

ARNIE'S ARMY

The phrase "Arnie's Army" dates back to the 1960 Masters, when soldiers from nearby Fort Gordon followed Arnold Palmer around the course. Palmer was on his way to his second Masters victory with a 20-foot birdie putt at the 17th and a four-foot birdie putt at the 18th when an "Arnie's Army" sign appeared on the giant back-nine scoreboard.

Grassroots enlistment into Arnie's Army actually began in 1958. The Masters was not a sellout in those early years. Clifford Roberts, Augusta National's cofounder, used soldiers from the nearby military training base to work the scoreboards and act as gallery marshals. He also wanted a large crowd since the Masters was being televised for the third time, so he gave free passes to any soldier who showed up in uniform. Most of the soldiers were not golf aficionados; they simply wanted to spend a day off base among the dogwoods and azaleas. Over the first three rounds, as Palmer fearlessly played his way into a tie for first place with Sam Snead, he won over the troops and most of the crowd. The Sunday gallery, estimated at more than 30,000—a Masters record—stormed the gates to inspire a Palmer coronation.

Autograph seekers at Congressional Country Club in Washington, D.C., besiege Palmer after he completed a practice round in preparation for the 1964 U.S. Open. (AP Photo)

For his part, Arnold wasn't about to disappoint the soldiers or fans by playing it safe down the stretch. A nascent army was unofficially born. Their support helped carry Arnold to a rousing victory.

Recruitment into Arnie's Army got a big boost during the 1959 Masters. Joining Arnold's gallery from the start, the soldiers rallied around the charismatic defending champion who had won his first major a year earlier at Augusta National. Arnold shared the lead entering the final round, but his chances for back-to-back tournament titles met their doom when he triple-bogeyed the 12th hole. Never one to raise a white flag, Arnold fought valiantly over the final six holes but came up two strokes short. His no-surrender ethos resonated with the military men and civilians alike.

> ## "When people ask what's driven me all these years, I always give the same answer. It's you." —Arnold Palmer

Undeterred, Arnie's Army returned in force the following year, throwing their full-throated support to the 30-year-old U.S. Coast Guard veteran. While Palmer was rallying in spectacular fashion to win his second green jacket in 1960, battalions of his supporters were poised for a victory celebration. They maneuvered to the flanks of the 18th green to witness the decisive shot. That prompted one of the GIs working a back-nine scoreboard to announce the arrival of "Arnie's Army" with a handwritten sign, which is what the scene looked like with all those men in uniform.

"I can't remember another time, other than my stint in the Coast Guard, when so many uniformed soldiers surrounded me," Arnold recalled.

A soldier looks on as Palmer receives a smooch from Miss Golf during the 1959 Masters. (AP Photo)

Johnny Sands, a copyeditor for the *Augusta Chronicle*, picked up on the phrase and ran the headline "Arnie's Army," for the first time putting a name to the movement. By gosh, did the term ever stick in the sports lexicon. Every newspaper, magazine, and television station that covered golf adopted the moniker. Arnold reached national cover boy status, appearing on the May 2, 1960, cover of *Time* as a player who is "boldly ushering in" a new era of golf.

Soon, nonuniformed fans across the land enlisted in the golfing army. In 1960, during the U.S. Open at Cherry Hills in Denver, the gallery was in Arnold's corner like never before. As Palmer was making his miraculous charge, it seemed as if everyone on the grounds was rooting for him to win.

"The cheers of the crowd that day will always be among my greatest memories," he said. "I know the support of Arnie's Army had as much to do with my winning the championship as the shots I played."

In 1960, Arnold was at the top of his form, winning eight of the 27 tournaments he entered, including the

A soldier in Arnie's Army wore this vintage pin. (Authors' Collection)

Fans in a high perch glimpse Arnold Palmer during the Ryder Cup, at Royal Lytham & St. Annes, on October 14, 1961. His three match wins helped the U.S. team defeat Britain. (AP Photo)

Masters and the U.S. Open. He was the PGA Tour's leading money winner and was the first professional golfer to earn more than $75,000 in a single season. Culminating a seminal year on tour, he was voted winner of the Hickok Belt as the top pro athlete of the year. *Sports Illustrated* named Arnold Palmer its 1960 Sportsman of the Year, the first golfer so honored.

***

In 1962, after winning his third Masters title, Palmer thanked the "army" of supporters who came out to follow him. By then, Arnie's Army had turned into a revolution.

Almost everywhere he played, Palmer's mobilized force of fans was there to cheer him on. At the British Open in Scotland in 1962, his militia ratcheted up the noise to a level that echoes to this day. By the 11th hole in the final round, Arnold had stampeded his way to a 10-stroke lead. What must have been one of the wildest galleries in golf history was joyously stampeding with him. The

Gallery favorite Palmer, front and at right of caddie No. 71, strides down the hill of the 8th fairway with a huge crowd behind him during third-round play of the 1963 Los Angeles Open. (AP Photo)

enthusiastic mob of 15,000 Scots was swollen beyond all control. Hordes of people swarmed the Old Troon course unrestrained, thundering their way toward Arnold in the hopes of getting close to him. He had to fight his way through a throng of these invaders on every fairway just so he could reach the ball.

Palmer had become "something of a worldwide sporting Beatle," noted writer Dan Jenkins.

It took a phalanx of policemen to wedge him through the pushing, hollering mass of people around the 18th green. The crowd, seemingly on the verge of riot, formed a scary wall of noise. Television cameras were unable to locate Arnie from amongst the crowd. When a broadly smiling Palmer finally came into view, he staggered in a mock limp of exhaustion onto the 18th green.

"You could not find a more popular man in all of Scotland," said a relieved television broadcaster.

With peace restored, Arnold proceeded to sink a birdie putt to finish his four-day assault on the Scottish links with a total of 276. His six-stroke cushion over Australian Kel Nagle was the biggest victory margin in any British Open since 1929 and the best score in Open history to that point. It was Palmer's second consecutive win in the British Open, and the frenzy triggered by his repeat at Royal Troon prompted the authorities to institute more rigorous crowd control measures in every Open to follow. Roping off fairways and fencing course boundaries began a year later at Royal Lytham & St. Annes, host of the 1963 Open Championship, and has been the norm ever since.

There were occasions, however, when his army's enthusiasm crossed the line. Such a time was the 1962 U.S. Open at Oakmont Country Club outside Pittsburgh.

"You'd better watch the fat boy," Arnie had warned writers before the tournament.

He was referencing an up-and-coming rookie pro from Ohio named Jack Nicklaus, who ventured into hostile Pennsylvania Palmer Country ready to take on the local hero. Arnold's rowdiest boosters would purposely mispronounce the young Buckeye's name as Nick-louse or Nick-loss. The worst of the abuse was directed at Nicklaus during the playoff. Hecklers held signs over bunkers exhorting him to "Hit it Here, Fat Boy," and the riled-up crowd stomped in unison while he putted.

In what many consider a major turning point in golf's transfer of power, the young Nicklaus beat Palmer in that U.S. Open playoff to win the first of his record 18 majors. Afterward, Palmer apologized to Nicklaus for the crowd's unruly behavior. Nicklaus told him he understood, but the treatment had affected him.

"Arnold played a role in my growing up," he told Palmer biographer Thomas Hauser. "It wasn't easy. In fact, it was very tough for me to compete against Arnold and his gallery."

***

Even when Arnold Palmer lost, his army did not desert him. In the 1961 Los Angeles Open at Rancho Park, he recorded a 12 on the par-5 18th hole. He hit four balls out of bounds, kicking away the tournament. Palmer and his loyal fans were deflated, but not for too long. Asked by a reporter

Arnold tees off during the PGA Championship at Aronimink Golf Club in Newtown Square, Pennsylvania, on July 19, 1962. Jack Nicklaus, who beat him one month earlier at the U.S. Open, stands behind him. The pairing attracted the largest gallery in first-day play. (AP Photo/Bill Ingraham)

how he managed to make a 12, he replied, "I missed my putt for an 11."

Palmer didn't just play a golf course; he assaulted it.

"He goes right for the throat of a course," said fellow pro Jerry Barber, "and then he shakes it to death."

Arnie was human, a golfer who could blow a lead or shank a shot like any duffer. He visibly agonized over sliced drives and punched his fist into the air after sinking clutch putts. Fans loved it, even when he was not in contention.

"He was the Perils of Pauline," *Los Angeles Times* columnist Jim Murray wrote. "Every round was a cliffhanger. Continued next week."

Even with the ups and downs on the course, Palmer's popularity never waned. No matter where or when he played, his galleries were the largest and loudest, cheering every birdie with a loud "Charge!"

People liked that he went down swinging, booming big drives that might land buried in a ditch or fly beyond the cart path.

"I was often where they were as I came down the stretch," he said, "in the rough, the trees, or up the creek."

When he did hit a wayward tee shot to an awkward spot, he usually went for the green, rather than chip the ball safely back to the fairway, as other golfers would have done. This only bolstered his appeal to the average Joes.

Gary Player once suggested in *Golf Digest* that Palmer might have won more majors if he had been a little more conservative, but then he wouldn't have been Arnie.

Faithful fans stretch out along the 14th fairway of Augusta National to witness four-time Masters champion Arnold Palmer hit his driver, in 1965. (AP Photo)

"You can make mistakes when you're being conservative, so why not go for the hole?" Arnie said. "I always feel like I'm going to win. So I don't feel I'm gambling on a lot of shots that make other people feel I am."

***

Golf was still an antiquated game played by the country club elites when Palmer burst upon the scene, a young, dashing, daring, and even sexy matinee idol. He was to golf what John F. Kennedy was to politics: something the country had not seen before. Both famously benefited from the power of television. Palmer became a full-blown television sports star. He was Mickey Mantle in khakis, Frank Gifford in a polo shirt. Only Arnie was also approachable; no barriers separated him from his fans. He could be touched, literally, by the crowds that followed him and identified with his common man upbringing.

Palmer never lost his strong link to the regular, everyday people who were his devoted fan base. It was not uncommon for him to chat up bystanders and reporters as he walked the course. Once, when confronted with an ugly lie in the bunker, Palmer solicited advice from columnist Jim Murray.

"OK, Jim," Palmer said, "you're always writing about how great Ben Hogan was. What would Hogan do in a situation like this?"

Murray quipped: "Hogan wouldn't have been in a situation like this."

No matter the predicament, Arnie was never one to panic. He displayed many emotions on the golf course, but caution and fear were not among them. He captured the fancy of the public with his swagger. He would reach into his bag and pull out a club like a knight had drawn his sword. The quintessential Palmer mannerisms and his good looks—a bit of Errol Flynn, a dash of Elvis Presley—carried the game to an unprecedented surge of popularity. With the Cuban Missile Crisis dominating the news during the autumn of 1962, when Washington, D.C., and Moscow sparred right on the edge of thermonuclear war, many Americans looked to Arnie to help relieve the tension they were feeling.

Arnie lets loose a cheer with fans after sinking his 25-foot birdie putt at the 15th hole during the final round of the Kemper Open in Sutton, Massachusetts, on September 15, 1968. Palmer earned his 54th career title and a $30,000 first-prize check. (AP Photo/ Bill Chaplis)

Palmer flashes the $25,000 winner's check at the Thunderbird Classic in Harrison, New York, on June 16, 1963. He was the PGA Tour's leading money winner for a second straight year. (AP Photo/John Lindsay)

"Arnold Palmer didn't make golf," Murray wrote, "he just put it on Page 1."

In 1962, he was Player of the Year and earned more than $80,000 in purses, and he'd already won six major championships. Although Arnold did not win a major tournament in 1963, he won enough to become the first golfer to top the $100,000 mark in single-season winnings, finishing the year with $128,230. He made three times that much in endorsements. He was the envy of his fellow pros.

"We're all a little jealous of him," said longtime rival Chi Chi Rodriguez. "But golf without Arnie would be like *Gunsmoke* without Matt Dillon. There's no *Gunsmoke* without Matt Dillon."

On the list of major championship winners, Palmer sits in a five-way tie for seventh with seven triumphs—way behind Nicklaus's total of 18. Arnie won his first major in 1958 and his last in '64.

"Jack [Nicklaus] won majors for 25 years; I won them for 20; Arnold won them for six," Gary Player said. "But because he was so charismatic, because he did so much for golf, because the people loved him so dearly, they thought he was still winning. And, you know what? He was."

CHAPTER 5

THE PEOPLE'S CHAMP

On Easter Sunday, 1964, Arnold Palmer stood in the fairway of the par-5 Firethorn hole at Augusta National, pulling a 3-wood from his bag. He would attempt to clear the pond that fronted the green of 15. "Dave Marr looked at me as if I'd lost my mind," Palmer wrote in his autobiography, *A Golfer's Life.*

With just four holes to play in the Masters, Palmer knew he had a five- or six-shot lead. Any sane golfer would have played this hole safe. Lay up short of the green, pitch, and putt for a comfortable par, then cruise to victory over the last three holes. By all means, don't play he-man and try to clear the water, risking a drop into the drink and a sure 6, or maybe a 7.

Throughout his career, Arnie had lost many a tournament by playing too aggressively. Critics pointed out, and he agreed, that he had fallen short in three or four U.S. Opens, at least two PGA Championships, and one or two Masters by refusing to play it safe at certain points. Yet, if he hadn't *gone for it* as much as he did, "I wouldn't have won half the tournaments I did win," he wrote. "Going for the green in two was who I was as a boy—and it's who I remain as a man."

Palmer and his caddie try, unsuccessfully, to will in his eagle attempt on the 13th hole on Sunday at the 1964 Masters. Arnold won by six strokes to become the tournament's first four-time winner. (AP Photo)

So as the sun descended into the Georgia pines on this holiest of days, Palmer squinted into the glare and blasted his 3-wood with all he had. He lost sight of the ball and feared the worst, but the roar of the gallery settled his nerves. He had cleared the pond and could finally breathe easy at Augusta. He had won three green jackets prior to 1964, all requiring spectacular finishes. Now, having won the gamble at 15, he could enjoy his strolls along the remaining holes. He finished with a 12-under 276, six shots ahead of Marr and fellow runner-up Jack Nicklaus.

"This is the most singularly exciting tournament for me ever," Palmer said after becoming the first four-time winner of the Masters. "For once in my life, I planned to do something and did what I wanted."

Though growing wealthy from the game he loved—becoming the first golfer to reach $500,000 in career earnings with this Masters win—he didn't show it. While doling out thank-yous during the green jacket presentation, Arnie expressed his gratitude to "the members of the gallery, especially. They're my friends."

While his triumph at Augusta in 1964 was uncommonly smooth, Palmer's season as a whole—in fact, the whole rest of the decade—was rocky traveling. After leading the Tour in victories for four straight years (1960-63), he didn't win at all from October 1963 until the Masters in mid-April. He blamed his troubles on quitting cigarettes. "I had mental, or maybe you would say psychological, problems since I quit smoking," he told reporters at Augusta. "I have been jittery and I think my game showed it, but I think I have it licked now."

Palmer's drought paralleled the long, hard winter that America had just endured. President John F. Kennedy had been assassinated in November 1963, precipitating months of sorrow and gloom. Thankfully, the Beatles arrived in

Three days after winning the 1964 Masters, Arnie was back at his favorite place, his home in Latrobe, playing pool with his father, Deacon. (AP Photo/Dozier Mobley)

America in early 1964, scoring the top five spots on the Billboard charts in early April with such cheery songs as "I Wanna Hold Your Hand" and "Can't Buy Me Love." The Masters, as usual, signaled the arrival of spring, and Arnie's return to the winner's circle made many feel that all was right with the world again.

In terms of fame, golf income, and endorsements, Arnie was at the top of his game. But something happened to

Arnold, Winnie, and daughter Amy, age five, express the joy and love they felt on the grounds of their Latrobe home—as do dog Thunder and pony Zorro. (AP Photo)

Palmer mentally in 1964, a subject he dwelled on for several pages in *A Golfer's Life*. Doubt and fear crept into his mind. In critical moments, he was afraid of disappointing his followers by missing a shot, causing him to play certain holes safe.

In *Golf's 8 Second Secret*, acclaimed golf instructor Mike Bender writes about the importance of performing swiftly,

efficiently, and instinctively on the course, leaving no time for second-guessing (doubt) to set in. Bender studied film footage of the 18 greatest male golfers of all time, whom he defined as those who won at least five majors (including Palmer during his heyday). All but one of them performed their preshot phase (defined by Bender) in 12 seconds or less and their swing phase within eight seconds. All of them relied on instincts. Grip it and rip it. The nongreats took longer.

In hindsight, it's quaint to think that Arnie's downfall began because he didn't want to disappoint his fans—those who spent hard-earned money to see him live, whose face lit up when he gave them a wink, and in one case who flew an airplane with the sign "Go, Arnie, Go!" But for Palmer, it wasn't "quaint" at the time.

Palmer won just one more tournament in 1964, the Oklahoma City Open Invitational. He challenged in the other two American majors but inevitably fell short. In the U.S. Open, he trailed by just a shot after two rounds but, in intense heat at Congressional Country Club in Bethesda, Maryland, wilted on Saturday, shooting 75-74 to lose by eight strokes to Ken Venturi. With the temperature above 100 degrees and near 100-percent humidity, it "felt like a blowtorch was aimed at your neck," said competitor Raymond Floyd.

At the 1964 PGA Championship, Palmer trailed leader Bobby Nichols by just a shot entering the final round. Arnie played well on Sunday and actually became the first player ever to post four rounds in the 60s in a major championship (68-68-69-69), but he still lost by three to Nichols, whom Palmer called the "best scrambler I ever played against."

The numbers seemed to support what Palmer had admitted: that he was choking in the clutch. Arnie made the cut in each of his 26 PGA Tour events in 1964 and recorded 18 Top 10 finishes. He finished second in earnings with $113,203 (Nicklaus won with $113,285), and he even won

his third Vardon Trophy in four years by averaging 70.18 strokes per round. Yet, he won only the two tournaments, trailing Tony Lema (five), Nicklaus and Billy Casper (four), and Venturi (three).

While just $82 separated Nicklaus and The King in 1964, Jack staged the equivalent of a coup in '65. We can even pinpoint the day it happened: Saturday, April 10, at Augusta National. Entering the third round, the Big Three—Palmer, Nicklaus, and Gary Player—sat atop the leaderboard with 138s. While Palmer sputtered to a 72 on Saturday, the Golden Bear shot eight birdies and 10 pars to tie the course record with a 64. Nicklaus won the tournament the next day with a Masters-record 271 (-17), prompting Bobby Jones to utter the famous quote, "He plays a game with which I am not familiar." Arnie and Player tied for second, nine shots behind.

"He was Indiana Jones with a 5-iron. If Dumas were alive in the 20th century, that swashbuckler alongside the Three Musketeers wouldn't have been named D'Artagnan. It would have been D'Arnie." —Jeff Jacobs, *Hartford Courant*, September 26, 2016

That 1965 season turned out to be "a genuine torment from beginning to end," Palmer wrote. He no longer smoked, but he compensated for his cravings by eating more and putting on weight. In addition to his mental burdens, he suffered from bursitis in his shoulder for most of the year.

He won the Tournament of Champions on May 2 for his only victory of the year and finished 10th on the money list with $57,770, just over $82,000 behind Nicklaus, the top earner ($140,752).

While Palmer started to feel the effects of age—he turned 36 in the summer of 1965—the country was changing around him too. President Lyndon Johnson initiated Operation Rolling Thunder in March, a relentless bombing campaign of North Vietnam, and increased the US presence in Vietnam from 23,000 troops to 184,000. Young Americans—angry at the aggression, scared of the draft, and feeling restrained by the country's conservative Christian values—created their own counterculture, one based on "sex, drugs, and rock 'n' roll," not to mention long hair and fierce opposition to the war.

The golf world, and Palmer almost symbolically so, maintained its conservative nature, for better or worse. On the PGA Tour, a few golfers would begin to sport mustaches, longer sideburns, and *slightly* longer hair, though that all didn't happen until decade's end. More troubling was that the Tour remained almost entirely white, despite the civil rights movement struggle that raged during the 1950s and '60s, culminating in the Civil Rights Act of 1964 and Voting Rights Act of 1965—and then exploding into the urban riots of the mid- to late '60s.

Charlie Sifford broke the PGA Tour color barrier in 1961, but the Masters did not field a single black competitor until Lee Elder in 1975. The Masters was independent of the PGA Tour, and Augusta National members set the qualifications for invitation. Civil rights advocates noted that Masters champions were allowed to nominate a player who otherwise didn't qualify, meaning Palmer and others could have forced the racial issue. They did not. Author Howard Sounes writes in *The Wicked Game*, "Arnold Palmer takes the view that golf clubs can have any kind of membership policies they like. . . . By nature, he wanted to be everybody's friend and preferred to resolve such delicate matters in private."

Personally, Palmer was getting overwhelmed by golfing commitments. Increasingly, he had filled his off-season with a growing number of big-money exhibition events and foreign tournaments. But in 1965, he and Winnie felt he should simplify his schedule and rest more during the winter months. He enjoyed spending more time with his daughters and Winnie, and tinkering in his workshop.

In 1966, Palmer began the PGA Tour season like a new man, ripping off a personal-record seven birdies in a row in the third round of the Los Angeles Open for a 62, which propelled him to victory. After he forged three more top-three finishes, Arnie's Army believed their man was back. Palmer led the '66 Masters on Sunday and finished fourth, then led the U.S. Open at San Francisco's Olympic Club after three rounds. Unfortunately, he was about to suffer one of the most infamous collapses in golf history.

For the first time, the U.S. Open's final round began on Sunday. With just four holes to play, Arnie led by five shots over playing partner Billy Casper. Palmer tried to go for birdie at the 15th and landed in the sand, leading to a bogey while Casper birdied. On the 604-yard 16th, Arnie

Palmer chats with Dean Martin at the 1966 Bing Crosby Pro-Am in Pebble Beach, California. Arnie played with Deano several times and also knew Rat Packers Frank Sinatra and Sammy Davis Jr. (AP Photo)

landed in deep rough and bogeyed, while Casper holed another birdie putt, cutting the lead to one.

Olympic Club member Rita Douglas remembered walking with Winnie during the later holes. "Her poor little face kept getting sadder and sadder," Douglas told ESPN.com.

"Winnie was always smiling on the golf course, but she couldn't smile that day."

Palmer left a seven-foot putt an inch short on 17, cringing at the outcome, then headed to 18 tied for the lead. "Palmer was famous for making eye contact with one and

Ominously, in the final round of the 1966 U.S. Open, Palmer misses his birdie putt on the 14th hole. His epic collapse would begin with a bogey on 15. (AP Photo)

all, for making sure the crowds felt they were part of his experience," Ian O'Connor wrote on ESPN.com. "But as his world spun out of control, Palmer disconnected from the fans. On the 18th green he was a dark, solitary figure lurching over a downhill, left-to-right 4-footer he needed to qualify for a playoff."

He made the putt to enter an 18-hole Monday playoff, and he led that round by two after nine . . . only to shoot 40 on the back nine and lose by four.

"There is a picture of us walking off the 18th green and I've got my arm around Arnold's shoulder," Casper recalled. "I told him, 'I'm sorry, Arnold.' And I meant it."

Despite the heartbreaking defeat, Palmer had rebounded from his troubled 1965 season and enjoyed a terrific year. In 1966 he won the Tournament of Champions and the Houston Champions International, triumphed in the Australian Open, and partnered with Nicklaus to capture the PGA Team Championship and the Canada Cup.

An ecstatic Palmer runs his hands through his $20,000 winnings at the 1966 Tournament of Champions in Las Vegas. Tournament Chairman Allard Roen (left), tourney queen Jean Carroll, and runner-up Gary Brewer share in the joy. (AP Images/Harold Filan)

Palmer excelled despite a seemingly exhausting schedule of appearances and endorsements, requiring the assistance of his full-time pilot, Darrell Brown, and full-time administrative assistant, Doc Griffin. In September 1966, Arnie's appeal reached the highest of levels when President Lyndon Johnson requested that he visit the White House. Burmese dictator General Ne Win, an avid golfer, was visiting, and LBJ hoped that Palmer could stop by and butter up the powerful visitor, whose support Johnson coveted for the war effort. Arnie couldn't attend, but a State Department official and US senators immediately urged him to stage a golf exhibition in Thailand, Cambodia, and Malaysia to win hearts and minds in the region.

Palmer finally got some time to relax on September 10, his birthday. He was enjoying a quiet day at home when the doorbell rang. "Answer it, Arn," Winnie said, as recalled by Palmer's attorney Mark McCormack. "It's the TV repairman." Arnie answered and there stood—whaddaya know?—former President Dwight Eisenhower. Unbeknownst to her husband, Winnie had invited Ike and former First Lady Mamie for the weekend. Eisenhower didn't come empty-handed, providing Arnie with a farm scene that he had painted. The 37-year-old birthday boy and the savior of the free world went golfing that day, and then they all enjoyed a small dinner party, which included George Love, chairman of the board of Chrysler.

***

In 1967, Palmer experienced his last year as an elite-level competitor. He won four PGA Tour events: the L.A. Open,

Two American heroes, Palmer and President Dwight Eisenhower, were best of friends. They enthralled each other with their stories— Arnie from the links, Ike from the warfront. (AP Photo)

Tucson Open, American Golf Classic, and Thunderbird Classic. He also prevailed in a memorial event for Tour veteran Tony Lema, who had died in a plane crash the previous summer. In that event, Palmer shot a course-record 63 at the Stardust Country Club in Las Vegas, beating runner-up Bobby Nichols by seven shots. "The wind was howling that

In this *Sports Illustrated* issue, dated March 6, 1967, attorney Mark McCormack details the busy business life of the sports world's most marketable star. (Authors' Collection)

day, up to 30 miles per hour," Nichols said. "It's one of the most incredible rounds of golf Arnold ever played."

Arnie placed fourth at Augusta, wound up second in the U.S. Open (four shots back of Nicklaus at Baltusrol), and finished second on the money list with $184,065, less than five grand behind Jack. His fourth and final Vardon Trophy was proof of Arnie's consistent excellence. He also won the Piccadilly World Match Play Championship, the World Cup with partner Nicklaus, and the individual World Cup International Trophy.

"Arnold had hands like Rocky Marciano. When he closed his fist, it must've weighed 10 pounds."
—Chi Chi Rodriguez

Never again would Palmer achieve such glory. In 1968 he won another early-season event, the Bob Hope Desert Classic, beating Deane Beman in a playoff—much to the delight of Bob himself. Palmer had made a cameo in a screwball Hope comedy film, *Call Me Bwana* (1963), and he would appear on his television shows over the years. Hope often used Palmer as a vehicle for one of his dumb golf jokes. "There are two things that made golf appealing to the average man—Arnold Palmer and the invention of the mulligan," he once quipped to obligatory laughs.

At Augusta in April 1968, which began seven days after Martin Luther King Jr. was assassinated, startling events happened at the Masters. Argentinian Roberto DeVicenzo seemingly was headed to a playoff with Bob Goalby, but

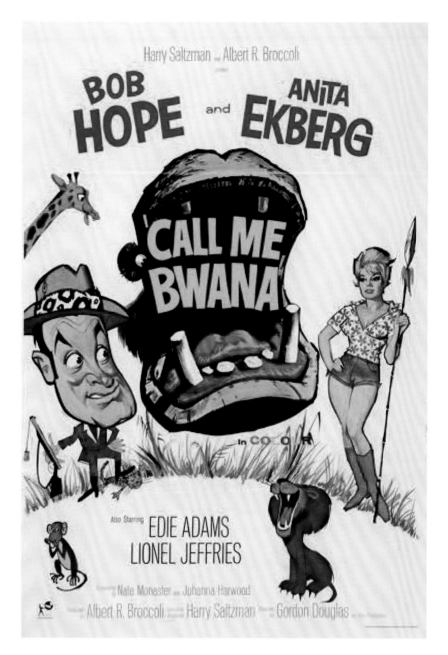

Palmer appeared in the 1963 Bob Hope film *Call Me Bwana*, bumping into the comedian on a golf course in an African jungle. (Heritage Auctions)

At the 1968 Masters, Palmer looked debonair in his blue turtleneck and sweater, but his golf game that week wasn't as sharp. He shot 72-79, missing the cut in that tournament for the first time. (AP Photo)

playing partner Tommy Aaron had written a 4 for the 17th hole (instead of the correct 3) on DeVicenzo's scorecard and Roberto signed it, making it official. Goalby thus prevailed. "What a stupid I am!" DeVicenzo said. Just as shocking, Arnold Palmer missed the cut. He splashed water three times on Friday for a 72-79. Over the previous 10 years, Arnie had won the Masters four times and posted two seconds, a third, and two fourths.

Eerily, the 1968 U.S. Open began seven days after Senator and presidential frontrunner Bobby Kennedy was assassinated. Oak Hill Country Club in Rochester, New York, played tough, with only winner Lee Trevino and Jack Nicklaus breaking par. Palmer made the cut but perhaps wished he hadn't, finishing in 59th place at 21 over par. Still, his Army remained loyal, and he even garnered a new recruit: Trevino.

"The highlight of that week was meeting Arnold Palmer for the first time," recalled the young "Merry Mex." "I was sitting there signing my card and he came over, shook my hand, and said, 'Nice going, young man.' Man, that was something."

The PGA of America decided to stage the 1968 PGA Championship in San Antonio in the middle of July, and—wouldn't ya know?—it was scorching hot. It was so hot that Trevino woke up parched late Saturday night and started chugging Gatorade that he found in a refrigerator. It turned out that it was mixed with tequila. "I woke up blind drunk," Trevino said. He then shot a 76.

Palmer, meanwhile, was stone sober, "playing beautifully and hitting some of his finest shots in years," wrote Dan Jenkins in *Sports Illustrated*. Unfortunately, Palmer missed a 12-foot birdie attempt on the 72nd hole to lose by one to 48-year-old Julius Boros, who to this day remains the oldest winner of a major. For Palmer, it was his second of three second-place finishes in the only major he never won. With his second-place paycheck, Arnie became the first PGA Tour player to exceed $1 million in career earnings.

Palmer won the 1968 Kemper Open in September but wouldn't make sports headlines for another year. In September 1969—after the moon landing in July and just before the "Miracle" Mets' World Series victory—Palmer turned 40, but he still believed in himself. That month, he shot the lowest round of his life, 60, albeit at the Latrobe Country Club. That fall, Arnie was doing 100 sit-ups a day to help compensate for an old hip injury and was "in a very pleasant frame of mind about his golf—," wrote Dan Jenkins in *Sports Illustrated*, "almost as if he had reconciled himself to the fact it would all come back sooner or later if he only stopped pressing so hard and worrying about it."

On November 30, Palmer prevailed at the first Heritage Golf Classic, staged on the Nicklaus-designed Harbour Town Golf Links on Hilton Head Island, South Carolina. "It was like winning my first tournament," he effused afterward. A week later, Arnie charged from six strokes back on Sunday for a 65 to win the Danny Thomas-Diplomat Classic. "I knew I'd be back," he said after the victory. Palmer had thus closed the decade like he had begun it at Cherry Hills in 1960—as the most dynamic competitor in golf.

***

Early in 1970, Associated Press sportswriters and broadcasters voted Palmer the Athlete of the Decade. He received 231 of 655 votes, beating out such American icons as Bill Russell (194 votes after winning nine NBA championships in the decade for Boston), Sandy Koufax (56), Johnny Unitas (47), and Mickey Mantle (43), with Willie Mays, Bart Starr, Jim Brown, Wilt Chamberlain, and Bobby Hull rounding out the top 10. It says something about the conservative nature of the press at the time that Palmer breezed to the award while Muhammad Ali—the vocal opponent of the Vietnam War and *Sports Illustrated*'s Sportsman of the Century—didn't make the top 10.

"Arnold had a great ability to look you in the eye, sign an autograph and he made you feel like you were the only person in the world that he was dealing with at that moment."
—Andy North

Palmer, who had grown accustomed to high accolades, said, "This is quite an honor. Really an honor. I'm very pleased." He then returned to the topic of his golf game. "If I can keep my legs and back in shape, I can keep on going for some time yet," he said. "I can go on from here."

Arnie's Army wished he would go on decades. In many ways, he would.

CHAPTER 6

UNDER THE UMBRELLA

On Sunday, August 28, 1966, Arnold Palmer simmered with anger. He had just shot a 74 at the Philadelphia Open, and he blamed his poor performance on his relentless extracurricular schedule. "Mark, it's got to stop," he told Mark McCormack, his attorney and business manager. But it wouldn't stop anytime soon. Obligations awaited.

As McCormack recalled in a *Sports Illustrated* article, Palmer hopped into his personal Jet Commander plane that afternoon and was flown to New York City. On Monday he filmed a Noxzema commercial, and on Tuesday he flew to Shawnee, Pennsylvania, for the grand opening of a food-processing plant built by Winnie's father. On Wednesday, he flew back to New York, picked up four bigwigs from U.S. Banknote Corporation, and then golfed and dined them at Laurel Valley Golf Club. The next day, he posed for photographs for the Bolens Division of FMC, for whom he endorsed lawn equipment and snowplows.

On Sunday, he visited the Bluegrass State, where he was named a Kentucky colonel and played a golf exhibition, and the next two days he hosted 14 executives at Latrobe

during Arnold Palmer Enterprises days. That brings us to September, when LBJ invited to him to the White House (he was too busy to attend) and ol' Ike stopped by his Latrobe house for his birthday.

While John Lennon claimed that the Beatles were bigger than Jesus during the summer of 1966, Palmer was bigger than the Beatles—at least in the eyes of many sports fans and advertisers. Frank Chirkinian, a golf producer for CBS Sports, once said Palmer "had more charisma than any 10 guys I ever met. Maybe more than any 100."

McCormack helped Arnie turn his fame into a fortune. According to Forbes.com, Palmer earned $3.6 million in prize money during his 52 years on the PGA Tour and Champions Tour, and $875 million from appearances, endorsements, licensing, and golf course design. Among athletes, only Michael Jordan and Tiger Woods have amassed greater sums during their lifetimes.

During the 1950s, Arnie had been making just a few grand a year in endorsements. Winnie was his secretary and business manager, paying bills, balancing the books, and making travel arrangements. Then, late in 1959, Arnold

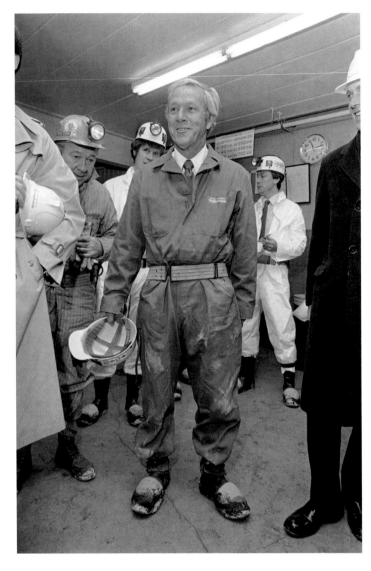

Palmer comes out of a Washington County mine on December 10, 1980, during a business tour of Pennsylvania. Arnold was the official spokesman for the state's new economic development advertising campaign. (AP Images/Bill Lyons)

signed with McCormack. In 1960 McCormack founded the sports agency IMG, and Palmer captivated the nation with his televised wins in the Masters and U.S. Open. In 1961, McCormack helped him establish Arnold Palmer Enterprises, Inc., a company with extraordinary marketing potential. But before they could launch, they needed a logo.

> **"Arnie was the most athletic, energetic, exciting golfer ever. Whether he's the best was irrelevant."**
> **—Russ Meyer, a cofounder of IMG and longtime Palmer confidant**

According to legend, Arnie and his business boys were sitting around a conference table, frustrated in their attempts to think of a logo. They considered crossed golf clubs, laurel leaves, and other ideas that were either trite or already trademarked. Needing a breather, Arnie went outside, where—amid a rainstorm—he saw a woman get out of her car and open a multicolored umbrella. The light bulb popped on. He returned to the conference room and said, "What about an umbrella?"

A multicolored umbrella—red, white, yellow, and green—became the official Arnold Palmer logo, and it remains so to this day. The logo is especially recognized in Asia, where there are 500 Arnold Palmer-branded stores.

In 1961, Palmer's off-course earnings skyrocketed to $500,000. ESPN noted that Palmer "endorsed Heinz

Arnold Palmer's Indoor Golf Course included a miniature Arnie and a club that featured an adjustable trigger mechanism. Players could drive off the tee, chip off the carpet, and putt into the hole. (Authors' Collection)

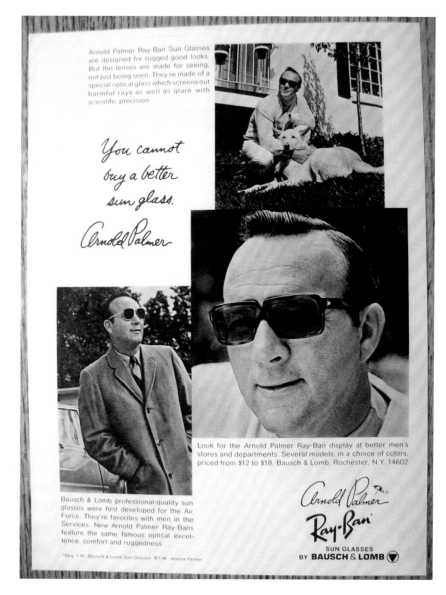

Arnold Palmer Ray-Bans could make even a small-town boy like Arnie look sexy and suave. (Authors' Collection)

ketchup on a steak, L&M filter cigarettes, Allstate insurance, Pennzoil motor oil, cardigans, dinner jackets and even Japanese robes." He represented Callaway, United Airlines, Coca-Cola, Rolex, Cadillac, Hertz, and many other companies. Early print ads reveal Arnie pitching the Apeco Super-Stat copy machine, Munsingwear golf shirts, Ray-Ban sunglasses, Sears golf clubs, a Bolens Husky riding lawn mower, Lanier's VestPocket Secretary (tape recorder), an indoor golf game, Woodward furniture, and Vycron polyester fiber.

Palmer ran a chain of dry cleaners, and as early as the late '60s he had offices in Latrobe; New York; Cleveland Chattanooga; and Pleasantville, New Jersey. In Tokyo, the Japanese dined happily in Tea Room Arnie.

As the representative of Palmer, Jack Nicklaus, and Gary Player, McCormack sought ways to promote the Big Three. In 1964, *Big Three Golf* ran on NBC for eight episodes. Palmer not only had a financial stake in the series, but the trio battled for hefty prize money, as well—all the while playing at such renowned locales as Los Angeles Country Club and the Old Course of St. Andrews. Amid the stress of travel and competition, the Big Three often let loose. Arnie recalled someone accidentally spilling a drink, triggering an all-out food and beverage fight.

Despite all his corporate affiliations and worldly travels, Palmer remained small-town at heart. "It is not so much that Arnold has an unquenchable love for Latrobe as that the things Latrobe represents are fundamental to his nature," McCormack wrote. "…He is at heart a man of enormous simplicity, of steak and *Bonanza*. (I remember

United's table-for-two Coach seating. For the champ. And her husband.

Winnie & Arnold Palmer aboard a United 727.

When Arnold Palmer faces competition as tough as this, he needs extra room to plan his next move. And United's table-for-two seating in Coach offers room enough for a champion. No matter how long it takes her to say "gin."

On many flights, when the center seat is free just one easy move makes it your own table-for-two. United has also provided additional closet space on board for those garment bags you might be carrying. We're helping to iron out the

wrinkles of long distance travel. And one quick call is all it takes to put you aboard. So tell your Travel Agent you want to be dealt a helping hand in the friendly skies. Or call United. And fly where the deck is stacked in your favor.

The friendly skies of your land.
United Air Lines
Partners in Travel with Western International Hotels.

Though he typically flew in his own planes, Arnold (and Winnie) helped plug United Airlines. He was the ideal choice for their "friendly skies" campaign. (Authors' Collection)

once years ago seeing him wave his spoon in annoyance because Winnie had put croutons in it.)"

While you couldn't take the Latrobe out of Arnie, you could upgrade it. By the late '60s, the Palmers expanded their home, adding on to the white two-story house with black shutters that overlooked the golf course. Additions included a garage, office, guest bedroom, game room, and workshop for Arnie, as well as a new dining room and kitchen. A dog named Thunder as well as a full-time secretary, Patty Aikens, kept Winnie and daughters Peggy and Amy company. When Arnie was home, his pilot, Darrell Brown, and administrative assistant, Doc Giffin, were often around. Giffin, a former newspaper reporter, would remain Arnie's right-hand man into their 80s. "I almost feel like a brother to Arnold," Doc said.

Throughout the turbulent '60s, the hippie '70s, the greedy '80s, and beyond, many Americans longed for the "good old days," typified by icons like Palmer. Advertisers honed in on his Americana charm, such as in a 1980s Pennzoil commercial. Set on an idyllic hole at Latrobe, Arnie appears with a tractor that seems to date back to the Coolidge administration. Arnie fires up the rickety machine and, before motoring off, says, "You know, this old tractor and I are a lot alike. We're both still using Pennzoil, and we're both still running."

Late in life, Palmer was still raking in the dough. In 2016, ArnoldPalmer.com listed his commercial partners, which included Callaway, Cessna, E-Z-Go Golf Carts, Golf Channel, *Golf Digest*, Insperity, Ketel One Vodka, *Kingdom Magazine*, Lamkin, and Rolex. Arnie was one of the founders of the 24-hour *Golf Channel*, flipping a ceremonial switch to launch the network on January 17,

Palmer's Swing after-shave "is bold and brisk," the ad declares, "...lots of authority. But never perfumy. Never weak and watery. Try Arnie's idea of a real man's after-shave." (Authors' Collection)

1995. The network struggled early on but decided to persevere, thanks in part to Palmer's encouragement. In the early days, the question arose whether investors should

CONSISTENT CLASSICS: PALMER AND ROLEX
The look is legend. Without peer and "better than par" in a lifetime of tournament golf. Arnold Palmer's game means style, performance, staying power. As does his timepiece, the Rolex Day-Date' Chronometer in 18kt. gold with matching, hidden-clasp President' bracelet, self-winding and pressure-proof down to 330 feet in its seamless Oyster' case. Like Arnie, unmistakable.

ROLEX

sidney mobell
Designer and Creator of Fine Jewelry

TWO FINE STORES IN SAN FRANCISCO
141 POST STREET · (415) 986-4747
FAIRMONT HOTEL · ATOP NOB HILL

Palmer's relationship with Rolex lasted more than 30 years. He also promoted other high-end products, including Cadillacs. (Authors' Collection)

WOW!
(You've just won Arnie for a day.)

Introducing the Arnold Palmer/Robert Bruce' Sweepstakes...your chance to win a day on the course with America's favorite golfer. Plus a full week's expense paid vacation for two at Arnie's Bay Hill Country Club in Orlando, Florida or Ironwood Club in Palm Desert, California.

Whether you need a few tips on your putting or have never held a club, you'll have the benefit of Arnie's expert instruction.

If your name is drawn first, you'll be our grand prize winner. If you're not quite so lucky, you may still win any of 200 other great prizes of Arnold Palmer sportswear.

All you do to enter is fill out the coupon below and deposit it in the official entry box in the men's sportswear department of any participating store. (For the name of the one nearest you, call toll-free from anywhere in the U.S. except Alaska and Hawaii 800-243-6000 anytime. In Connecticut call 1-800-882-6500.)

Of course it's all a plot to get you to see the entire line of Arnold Palmer sweaters and sweater-shirts by Robert Bruce featuring *DuPont fibers of Orlon*' acrylic and Dacron'* polyester. We're betting that once you've seen it, you'll understand why Arnold Palmer sportswear is the uncontested winner for good looks and comfort—on or off the course!

Arnold Palmer/Robert Bruce Sweepstakes Entry Form

Name..
Address..
City................State..........Zip.........
Participating Store.............................
Sweater/Shirt Size............................

Valid only when deposited in official "Arnold Palmer/Robert Bruce Sweepstakes" entry box in any participating store before June 10, 1977. Drawing will be held on July 15, 1977 in New York City under the auspices of the Public Relations Corporation of America. A list of major prize winners will be supplied upon written request accompanied by a postage prepaid return envelope submitted to Robert Bruce, "C" & Westmoreland Sts. Philadelphia, Penna. 19134, not later than December 31, 1977. Contest is open to residents of the U.S. only. All employees of Robert Bruce, Arnold Palmer Enterprises, Consolidated Foods and their advertising agencies and members of their immediate families are ineligible. Entrants must be 18 or older. Void where prohibited by law.   *DuPont TM

The winner of this sweepstakes could win a day on the golf course with Arnie at Bay Hill Country Club in Orlando, courtesy of Robert Bruce Apparel. (Authors' Collection)

ALL CLASS. ALL STYLE. ALL ARNIE. Introducing the Arnie Collection. A winning collection of fine fabrics and careful tailoring. Dress for work in three-piece, wool-blend suits,* dress slacks, shirts and ties. Dress for play in sport shirts, blazers, slacks and sweaters. Try on the New Arnie Collection. It's the master's touch.

Suits $150. Sport coats and blazers $95. Sweaters $30. Slacks from $29. Knit shirts $20. Available in most larger Sears retail stores. *55% polyester, 45% wool. ©Sears, Roebuck and Co. 1983.

Arnie ™

YOU'RE IN FOR A CHANGE AT Sears

This handsome Sears ensemble dates to 1983. Thirty-three years later, Sears.ca (Canada) was still selling Arnold Palmer apparel. (Authors' Collection)

cut their losses. "I said, 'Let me say this to you: If I didn't try to hit it through the trees a few times, none of us would be here." That quote is now on a wall at *Golf Channel* headquarters in Orlando.

**"It is not an exaggeration to say there would be no modern day PGA Tour without Arnold Palmer. There would be no PGA Tour Champions without Arnold Palmer. There would be no Golf Channel without Arnold Palmer."
—PGA Tour Commissioner Tim Finchem**

On *Golf Digest*'s list of highest paid golfers for 2015—on the course and off—Arnie ranked fifth with $40 million a year. He trailed only Jordan Spieth (first), Phil Mickelson, Tiger Woods, and Rory McIlroy, while edging out No. 6 Jack Nicklaus. On *Forbes*'s list of highest income for 2015 among retired athletes, Arnie ranked third with $42 million, behind Michael Jordan ($100 million) and David Beckham ($75 million).

MJ had the advantage of endorsing sneakers, but so did Palmer. In 2015, Nike came out with a LeBron James sneaker in Arnie's official logo colors: red, white, yellow, and green. They called the shoe the "LeBronold Palmer."

Arnie got into the wine business, selling Arnold Palmer Chardonnay and Arnold Palmer Cabernet Sauvignon. But he's known most for his iced tea and lemonade mix, a drink

As fans of the Arnold Palmer know, the lemonade sinks to the bottom while the iced tea rises to the top. (iStock by Getty Images)

famously known as the "Arnold Palmer." Not surprisingly, the story has humble origins. According to the man himself, Winnie was making iced tea one day when he told his wife, "Put a little lemonade in it and see how that works." It worked well.

The *naming* of the drink, the "Arnold Palmer," has its own charming story too—like a G-rated scene out of *When Harry Met Sally*. One day in the late 1960s, near Palm Springs, California, Palmer was ordering lunch and asked the waitress to mix lemonade with iced tea. A woman sitting nearby overheard the order and told the waitress, "I'll have that Arnold Palmer drink."

In 2001, Arnold Palmer Enterprises struck a deal with Innovative Flavors. While Arnie believed the drink should contain no more than one-third lemonade, the mass-marketed drink became known as "Arnold Palmer Half & Half: Iced Tea Lemonade." According to Golfweek.com, "In 2002 his company licensed AriZona Beverages to expand the distribution. It has grown from one product to more than 50, becoming nearly a $300 million wholesale business just in the U.S. in 2015."

Upon Palmer's passing, ESPN posted an old commercial online. Strolling through the ESPN cafeteria, Palmer stops at the drink section and fills his glass with iced tea… then with lemonade, while anchormen Stuart Scott and Scott Van Pelt curiously watch.

Hours after his passing on September 25, 2016, ESPN's SportsCenter sent out a tweet: "We"ll be having an Arnold Palmer for The King tonight."

Three cheers.

CHAPTER 7

DO NOT GO GENTLE...

Golf can be a tease to men in middle age. Since the sport rewards experience and doesn't require Olympic-level athleticism, golfers can still complete at a high level into their 40s. Even winning on the PGA Tour at that age is still possible, though only when the stars align.

Arnie's Army hoped that would be the case at the 1970 PGA Championship. Arnold Palmer, by then 40 years old with another birthday weeks away, found the ol' magic at Southern Hills Country Club in Tulsa, Oklahoma. Through three rounds of the only major he never won, Arnie was in third place, five shots behind leader Dave Stockton.

In a way, the differences between the two were amusing. Stockton, a rugged-faced, 28-year-old Californian, relied on cybernetics, the study of the automatic control system formed by the nervous system and the brain. Compare that to Arnie, the original grip-it-and-rip-it champion. All the while, Palmer searched for new ways to compete at his advanced age. He created a "cheat sheet" that included yardage and a diagram chart of the course. And he went with lighter woods for an easier swing without, hopefully, sacrificing distance. "I'm trying everything," he said.

On Sunday, though, it was Stockton who pulled a Palmer, sinking long putts and wedge shots on some holes while blowing up on others. In one stretch during the final round, Stockton shot birdie, eagle, double bogey, birdie. Palmer, meanwhile, consistently hit the greens for a smooth round of 70. Arnie's Army thought their hero had a chance until Stockton holed a 10-foot par putt on 17. He finished with a 73 and won by two over The King and Bob Murphy.

"I felt sorry for Arnold for about one-millionth of a second," Stockton said afterward, "because this is the only one he hasn't won."

And he never would win it. Throughout the 1970s—i.e., during his 40s—Palmer would see sporadic success. He would challenge in a few majors and win a handful of lesser events on Tour. But in what turned out to be a remarkably charmed life, Arnie would return to championship golf again in 1980, at age 50, the year he was eligible for the Senior PGA Tour—a tour that debuted that year and that he helped create.

Arnold's consistency helped him finish second in the 1970 PGA Championship, two shots back of Dave Stockton. Had he not double-bogeyed this hole, the 12th in the second round, he might have prevailed in the sole major he never won. (AP Photo)

Palmer won six PGA Tour events in the 1970s, including two in which he partnered with the reigning king of golf, Jack Nicklaus: the 1970 National Four-Ball Championship and the 1971 National Team Championship. He also prevailed in the 1971 Bob Hope Desert Classic, Florida Citrus Invitational, and Westchester Classic as well as the 1973 Bob Hope Desert Classic—his last Tour victory.

Palmer suffered serious putting woes in 1972, but he regained his touch in the '73 Hope event. On Sunday, a rainy day in the desert, Nicklaus had a chance to tie Arnie on the par-5 final hole, reaching the green in two. He could have potentially tied Palmer by knocking in the 30-foot putt, which he very nearly did.

"What are you trying to do?" Palmer asked Nicklaus.

"Trying to beat you," Jack replied.

Palmer then rolled in a seven-footer before tossing his visor in classic Arnie style.

Afterward, the winner's presentation got delayed when Hope couldn't find the giant $32,000 check.

"Who's got the money?" Hope asked.

"What are we going to do, just talk about it?" Palmer quipped. "Look, I really need the money. It's been a long dry spell."

The giddiness continued into the evening. That night, Jack donned a woman's wig and danced with Palmer cheek-to-cheek.

Though Arnold would never win another Tour event—and wouldn't crack the top 10 in the Masters during the '70s—he would prove remarkably competitive in the U.S. Open, finishing third, fourth, fifth, and ninth from 1972 to '75.

Young fans comfortably approach Palmer at the Bob Hope Desert Classic in February 1973. Arnold found his old putting stroke and won the tournament, his last-ever victory on the PGA Tour. (AP Photo)

In '72 at Pebble Beach, Palmer followed his opening 77 with a 68 on Friday. Or as author Ian O'Connor put it in *Arnie & Jack*, "Palmer came raging out of the past like an old lawman barreling through the swinging doors of a saloon." He trailed Nicklaus by just one shot after 68 holes, but Jack's iconic shot on the 17th, in which he hit the flagstick off the tee, sealed the victory. Arnie finished four shots back.

In the 1973 U.S. Open at Oakmont, Palmer paired the first two days with 26-year-old Johnny Miller, a long-haired blond from California. The gallery should have been gaga for the young hotshot, but instead Arnie's Army overran Miller's support. In fact, Miller said that playing amid the pro-Palmer crowd was like enduring a four-shot penalty.

Palmer actually shared the lead through three rounds (with Miller six shots back), and Arnie believed that he was leading while at the 11th hole on Sunday. Then he looked at the leaderboard and found that Miller was eight under for the day. "Where the [bleep] did he come from?" Arnie asked. Palmer went awry off the tee at the 12th while Miller—whose father had told him to go for broke, like Arnie—was on his way to a 63, becoming the first golfer to shoot that low in a major. Miller won at five-under; Palmer finished minus-three, tied for fourth with Nicklaus and Lee Trevino.

This 1970s Arnold Palmer golf bag sold for over $5,200 at auction. (Heritage Auctions)

"Playing with Mr. Pennsylvania at Oakmont in 1973 was an honor but also a challenge. Talk about chaos. If he made a 15-footer, the gallery didn't stick around to watch my 10-footer." —Johnny Miller, who nonetheless won the 1973 U.S. Open at Oakmont with a tourney-record 63

The 1974 U.S. Open was dubbed the "Massacre at Winged Foot" due to the brutality of the course. The

USGA made the test exceedingly difficult, players insisted, as revenge for Miller's 63 at Oakmont. No one broke par (70) the first day. Through Friday, four legends shared the top spot on the leaderboard: Hale Irwin, Raymond Floyd, Gary Player, and, yes, The King himself, Arnold Palmer, who opened 73-70. Early in his Saturday round, Palmer actually led by two strokes.

Not only was the crowd of 17,000 pulling for Arnie, ABC producer Chuck Howard got caught up in the dream. Irwin and Tom Watson pulled ahead on Saturday, prompting ABC director Jim Jennett to focus largely on them. But Howard, an ABC mainstay since Arnie's heyday in the early 1960s, kept urging Jennett to put Palmer on camera. "I couldn't figure out why," Jennett said. "He thought Arnold was going to snap out of it."

Palmer shot a 73 on Saturday, just three behind the leader, Watson. Irwin would prevail at plus-seven, five ahead of fifth-place Palmer. A 76 doomed Arnie on Sunday, but he left future *Golf Digest* editor Jerry Tarde with a memory he would never forget. "When Palmer came through 10, I was able to stand up [in the grandstand], turn around, and see him hit his tee shot," Tarde told ESPN.com. "A moment after I sat back down, there was this amazing eruption of cheers, and the grandstand literally shook. I stood up again to see what happened. 'Arnie holed it for a 2,' we heard. It was his last hurrah."

Refusing to "go gently into that good night," Palmer willed his way to an opening 69, two off the pace, in the 1975 U.S. Open at Medinah. He fell out of the top 10 with middle rounds of 75-73, but his closing 73 put him in a

Palmer misses a putt for par at the 11th hole in the 1975 U.S. Open at Medinah in Illinois. While he was not much of a factor on Tour during the mid-1970s, Arnold rose to the occasion in the U.S. Open, reeling off three top-five finishes from 1972 to '74 and losing by just three strokes in '75. (AP Photo)

tie for ninth—remarkably, just three strokes behind winner Lou Graham. Never again would Palmer finish better than 15th in a U.S. major, although he closed 67-69 at Turnberry in 1977 to finish seventh in the British Open.

In 1977, Arnie played in 21 PGA Tour events, the same number as he had in 1962, '65, and '66, but over the next two years he dropped down to 15 and 16. In '79, he finished in the top 25 only once, earning just $9,276. His putting touch had gone "in the tank," he said. Plus, he was "having fits with my vision, wrestling with eyeglasses and finally growing accustomed to wearing contact lenses." The ovations he heard from the gallery were for what he *had* accomplished as well as the occasional nice shot. The network cameras still cut to Arnie, but only for warm smiles and memories. He still made us feel good.

***

Always a workhorse, Palmer continued his business and leisure pursuits, including golf course design, flying airplanes, TV appearances, endorsements, and other business matters. His TV life had begun back in the '60s, when he appeared on the game shows *What's My Line?* and *I've Got a Secret*, as well as *Perry Como's Kraft Music Hall* and *That Regis Philbin Show*. Back in 1960, it took the *What's My Line?* panel a couple minutes to determine who he was, but in the '70s he was ubiquitous. Mike Douglas, his dear friend Dinah Shore, and Johnny Carson—whose career trajectory paralleled Palmer's—all had Arnie on their shows.

On July 17, 1970, Palmer actually guest hosted *The Tonight Show Starring Johnny Carson*, which back then was 90 minutes. His guests included crooner Vic Damone, lewd

Golf magazine touts Arnold's "power swing" in this June 1978 issue. (Authors' Collection)

comedian Buddy Hackett, and tennis great Rod Laver. In his 1999 autobiography, Arnie recalled how nervous he was that day and how "I'm hesitant to even go back and view the old tapes of the show."

Palmer and Winnie developed lasting friendships with Bob and Dolores Hope, iconic singer Bing Crosby, and prominent actors James Garner and Jack Lemmon. He hung out with Frank Sinatra, and President Kennedy sent him film of his golf swing expert analysis. Palmer is actually connected to most of the last 12 U.S. presidents, particularly Dwight Eisenhower.

Palmer first met Ike after winning the 1958 Masters, and after his '60 Masters win they developed a warm and long-lasting friendship. Eisenhower, who became serious about his golf game in retirement, at first hungered for tips from the game's best player, and Arnie happily obliged. One tip, though, wounded the retired five-star general. During an exhibition round, Palmer told Eisenhower to tuck in his right elbow during his swing. Ike, the good soldier, did as instructed and badly scraped his elbow on his metal-heavy belt, leading to a bloody shirt.

Eventually, Ike and The King dined and played cards together and conversed for hours, often at Augusta or at the Eisenhowers' cottage in Palm Desert, California. Both men were gentle-natured American heroes with similar ideologies, and they even had a similar countenance. "Arnold Palmer has what I call an 'Eisenhower smile,'" golf great Byron Nelson once said. "Those two men, they'd smile and their whole faces would look so pleasant; it was like they were smiling all over." The former president loved hearing about Palmer's PGA Tour life, and Arnie soaked in Ike's war stories. Palmer stated that his relationship with Eisenhower was stronger than with any older man besides his father.

Though a former member of Baltusrol Golf Club, President Nixon kept off the golf course during his presidency—an image that would not have looked good while young people were dying in urban riots and Vietnam. However, Nixon was enamored with both sports and celebrities—not just Elvis Presley, famously, but Arnold Palmer. Once during the Bob Hope Desert Classic, Nixon summoned Hope and Palmer to attend his San Clemente, California, home for a summit meeting about the Vietnam War. Palmer wondered *why me?*, but he was excited when a U.S. Marine helicopter flew Hope and him to San Clemente.

In Nixon's living room, Vice President Gerald Ford, Henry Kissinger, and others advised the president on how to end the war. Eventually, Palmer was asked for his input. "Well," he said, as he recounted in *A Golfer's Life*, "if the decision were mine to make, I guess I wouldn't pussyfoot around. Let's get this thing over as quickly as possible, for everyone's sake." And then he actually said, "Why not go for the green?" Everyone laughed at that, although Nixon would wind down as opposed to ramp up the war effort.

"Years back they were talking about Arnold running for senator and he could've won, he could've been the senator from Pennsylvania in 10 minutes. He could have been the governor of Pennsylvania, and if he'd have done that he probably would have ended up being the president."
—Andy North

In office for barely a month, President Gerald Ford tees it up with the Big Three (Palmer, Jack Nicklaus, and Gary Player) at Pinehurst Country Club in North Carolina, on September 11, 1974. Ford was known for his wayward drives into the galleries. (AP Images/Johnston)

Palmer attended multiple state dinners hosted by President Ronald Reagan, and he played golf on numerous occasions with Presidents Gerald Ford, George H. W. Bush, and Bill Clinton. On the day he left office, President Ford flew to California and partnered with Palmer at the Bing Crosby Pro-Am. Ford, Palmer said, was a powerful golfer but erratic (known for beaning members of the gallery). He rated Clinton as the best ball-striker among the presidents he had known, but he was too wild off the tee. "He can hit a long way," Palmer quipped. "He just doesn't have a ZIP code."

***

Palmer had great affection for President George H. W. Bush, whom he praised for his kindness, grace, "unpretentious charm," and "deep sense of honor." (AP Images/Doug Mills)

They called Yankee Stadium the "House that Ruth Built," not because he actually constructed the ballpark but because his popularity gave investors hope that it would it would be profitable. Similarly, you could call the Senior PGA Tour the "Tour that Palmer Built."

In the spring of 1979, the second annual Legends of Golf event excited NBC viewers, as the teams of Julius Boros/ Roberto De Vicenzo and Tommy Bolt/Art Wall burned up the Onion Creek course in Austin, Texas. Each team shot 15-under for 54 holes, then battled in a six-hole playoff that delayed the *NBC Nightly News*. Talk of a senior tour "started almost immediately because of the great show," pro golfer Bob Goalby told *Golf Digest*. "People said, 'Boy, those old bastards can still play.'"

Goalby knew that The King was going to turn 50 later that year. "I remember telling Art Wall, 'We're going to have a senior tour someday. The public is going to find a place for Arnold to play.'"

In January 1980, older players Boros, Goalby, Dan Sikes, Gardner Dickinson, Don January, and 67-year-old legend Sam Snead—who could still whack it—met with PGA Tour Commissioner Deane Beman about forming a senior tour. They all agreed that Palmer's involvement in the circuit was needed to lure sponsors. Arnie, still thinking he could compete on the PGA Tour, was conflicted about joining the old-geezers group. But he said yes for two reasons. One, he felt morally obligated to help out the friends and colleagues who had asked him for his support. Two, in December 1980 he prevailed in the 1980 PGA Seniors' Championship, a 50-and-older event that had been staged by the PGA of America since 1937. It felt "wonderful" to finally win again, Palmer said, and his victory excited corporate sponsors.

The 1980 PGA Senior Tour consisted of just four events, including the PGA Seniors' Championship and the inaugural U.S. Senior Open, which had an age limit of 55, thus excluding Arnie. Ratings for the event disappointed, so for '81 they dropped the qualifying age to 50. Palmer competed in the 1981 U.S. Senior Open at Oakland Hills and shot 289, tying him with Billy Casper and Bob Stone. That set up an 18-hole Monday playoff that sparked memories of the Palmer-Casper duel in the 1966 U.S. Open. This time, Arnie prevailed—another shot in the arm for the fledgling tour.

Palmer and Gary Player yuk it up at the 1986 Chrysler Cup in Potomac, Maryland. At these Senior PGA Tour events, winning was not as important as sharing laughs and stories—and maybe dinner afterward. (AP Photo)

The Senior PGA Tour grew from four events in 1981 to 11 in '82, of which Palmer won two. By 1988, the year of his 12th and final victory on the circuit, the Senior Tour had expanded to 34 events with $10,370,000 in prize money. The name was changed to the Champions Tour in 2003, a year in which the prize money rose to $53,600,000.

"They'd have to carry me out here before they would get me in a golf cart." —Arnold Palmer, after carts were permitted on the Senior Tour for the first time in 1985

Fans of the Senior Tour adored following their old faves, such as Lee Trevino and Chi Chi Rodriguez, who still slayed the bull/ball with his sword/putter. The circuit also allowed players to share laughs and stories with their old buddies while still competing in the game they loved.

To be sure, the events included many "senior" moments. "What's nice about our tour," said competitor Bob Bruce, "is you can't remember your bad shots."

The seniors could thank one ol' champion for making it all possible. . . . What was his name again?

CHAPTER 8

HIGHER PURSUITS

Arnold Palmer loved flying about as much as he hated driving. When he joined the PGA Tour in the mid-1950s, he and Winnie traveled to tournaments by car, hauling a nineteen-foot trailer that included a cramped kitchen, bedroom, and bathroom. That style of living got old fast.

"You don't realize how big our country is until you drive it," he once said. "On some of those longer jumps between tournaments, I almost literally climbed out of my car onto the 1st tee. All of that driving in the early years convinced me that flying was the only way to go."

As with television coinciding with his emergent popularity, and the Senior Tour beginning just after his 50th birthday, personal air travel took off just when Arnie needed it. Palmer had developed a love for flying as a youth by hanging around a small airport near Latrobe. In 1955 he started taking flying lessons in a single-engine Cessna 172 and soon began flying solo. In 1958 he leased a Cessna 175 and paid a copilot to fly with him, and in 1961 he purchased his first airplane, an Aero Commander 500. He bought bigger and faster planes over the years, allowing him and his entourage

to meet his business obligations even if they were halfway across the world.

> **"Flying has been one of the great things in my life. It's taken me to the far corners of the world. I met thousands of people I otherwise wouldn't have met. And I even got to play a little golf along the way."**
> **—Arnold Palmer**

Arnie's 20,000 flight hours included a few perks. He flew his Aero Commander alongside the Blue Angels, and he piloted such military aircraft as the DC-9, F-15, and F-16. He landed a military jet on the aircraft carrier *Eisenhower* (thankfully, he didn't miss that "green"!), and he test-flew a Boeing 747 and a McDonnell Douglas DC-10.

In May 1976, Palmer and his crew set an around-the-world flight record by circling the planet in 57 hours and 25 minutes. Arnie, two copilots, and a time observer landed

Palmer climbs out of his private jet plane in McKeesport, Pennsylvania, in May 1969. Arnie, who upgraded his aircraft numerous times, owned a Learjet and five different Cessna Citation jets. (AP Photo)

their jet in Denver after averaging 400 miles per hour and stopping in nine countries. They would have arrived sooner, but during their refueling stop in Sri Lanka, Arnold took time to ride an elephant.

For Arnie, the trip had felt like a long day at the office—Palmer style. "All I could think about was just getting back here," he said as a crowd of several hundred greeted him in Denver. Clean-shaven and looking well rested, Palmer gave Winnie a hug and then casually sipped champagne. "We lost some time because of headwinds, but otherwise things went just about as expected," he said, as if he had just carded a 70 at Augusta.

As he approached his 80th birthday, Palmer told Golf-Digest.com that he was still king of the skies. "I'm very current," he said. "I have another man who flies with me and we fly everywhere we go. You name it—from Europe and Hawaii. We do the whole thing." Never once, he said, in a half century of flying, did he ever face any dangers in the sky. A charmed life indeed.

"You know you're getting old when all the names in your little black book have M.D. after them."
—Arnold Palmer

***

Outside of his Tour play, Palmer's greatest legacy lay in golf course design. Incredibly, more than 300 Arnold Palmer designs dot the globe, in 35 U.S. states, 25 countries, and five continents (sans Africa and Antarctica).

As usual, the story of Palmer's design work has humble, charming origins. In 1963, the Latrobe Country Club featured just nine holes. Arnold and his father, Deacon, contributed heavily to the design of nine new holes and the revamping of the existing layout. The 6,377-yard, par-72 course opened in 1964. Arnold became sole owner of Latrobe Country Club in 1971, a year after claiming his stake on Bay Hill Club and Lodge in Orlando. The club's website states that Palmer "polished the original visions of Bay Hill into the opulent diamond it is today with the stature of a world-class facility." Palmer's Bay Hill course hosted a PGA Tour event every year, and in 2007 the name

was changed to the Arnold Palmer Invitational presented by MasterCard.

Arnie and his associates formed Palmer Course Design in 1972. "His early designs," wrote Golfweek.com's Bradley S. Klein, "emphasized elaborately shaped bunkering and the occasional photogenic beach bunker or bulk-headed peninsula green." However, Klein, noted, nobody "mistook Palmer for the architect. At news conferences and ribbon cuttings, Palmer would defer to his design associates to provide technical details."

Palmer's Bay Course at Kapalua Golf Club in Maui, Hawaii, opened in 1974. Whistler Golf Club in British Columbia (1980) and Tralee Golf Club in Ireland (1984) followed, and in 1985 he made history. That year, the Chung Shan Hot Spring Golf Club opened in Zhongshan City, China, becoming the first golf course ever in that ancient country.

In the 1980s and beyond, developers across the globe hungered for courses designed by either Jack Nicklaus or Arnold Palmer. In the 1990s, Palmer's design company in Ponte Vedre Beach, Florida, brimmed with activity, with more than two dozen employees managing 30-plus projects at once.

"I try to design golf courses that are individual in character and individual in their own standing," Palmer told Golf Digest.com. "An example would be, if someone came to me and they saw a golf course for the first time, and said, 'Yes. This is an Arnold Palmer golf course.' That wouldn't please me too much because we try to design courses that are not characteristic in any way. They are each individually designed. We try to do things different in every course we design."

Owned by Arnold Palmer since 1974, the Bay Hill Club has hosted the annual Arnold Palmer Invitational on the PGA Tour since 1979. (Arnold Palmer Design Company)

The Arnold Palmer Design Company has ventured boldly into China, designing courses such as this one at the Pure Scene Golf Club and Resort in Kunming. (Brandon Johnson/Arnold Palmer Design Company)

Notable efforts at the professional level include the Palmer Course at PGA National Resort and the Arnold Palmer Private Course at PGA West. Golf.com lists Palmer's 10 greatest designs as: Reunion Resort in Orlando; Turtle Bay in Oahu, Hawaii; Hiddenbrooke Golf Club in Vallejo, California; Half Moon Bay (Old Course) in Half Moon Bay, California; The Westin La Cantera (Palmer Course) in San Antonio; Deacon's Lodge in Breezy Point, Minnesota; Bay Creek Resort in Cape Charles, Virginia; Running Y Ranch in Klamath Falls, Oregon; Teton Pines in Wilson, Wyoming; and Tralee Golf Club in County Kerry, Ireland.

***

As a symbol of America itself—small-town, self-made, spirited, risk-taking—Arnold Palmer represented the United States on six Ryder Cup teams, in 1961, '63, '65, '67, '71, and '73. Palmer and the boys defeated Great Britain every one of those years, with Palmer winning 22 of his 32 matches to set a Ryder Cup record for most individual victories.

Arnold was ticked off that he didn't make the 1959 team, but the PGA rules indicated that he hadn't logged enough years on Tour to qualify. At his first Ryder Cup at Royal Lytham and St. Annes in 1961, he swelled with emotion. "I remember standing with my teammates near the first tee and feeling a lump rise in my throat and tears fill my eyes as the brass band played the 'Star-Spangled Banner' followed by 'God Save the Queen,'" he said on his website.

Palmer went 5-0 in the 1967 Ryder Cup in Houston, his only perfect performance, but it took the lure of a homemade clock to get there. In a four-ball match

In 1963, Palmer captained the U.S. team to a resounding 23-9 victory in Ryder Cup at East Lake Country Club in Atlanta. That year, he was the last playing captain in the event, for either side. (AP Photo/Horace Cort)

against Brits Hugh Boyle and George Will, Palmer and Julius Boros were three down. Jackie Burke—the five-foot-seven 1956 Masters champion and host professional at Champions Golf Club—started chiding Palmer, saying he didn't have faith that he and Boros could come back to win. Feeling challenged, Arnie wanted to bet Burke that they would indeed prevail. "I tell you what," Burke replied. "If you somehow get out of this mess and win this match, I'll make you a clock."

Palmer and Boros roared back to win by one, and Burke made good on his promise. One feature made the clock particularly unique: The handmade clock included 12 letters instead of the 12 numbers: A-R-N-O-L-D-P-A-L-M-E-R. Arnie found a special place for the clock in his workshop's office.

***

Arnold Palmer had the heart of a champion—the intense desire to not just win for himself, but to help as many people as he could. In the 1980s, he and Winnie committed to helping the women and children of Orlando, Florida, where the couple owned a winter home.

Back then, the region's population was booming, necessitating the need for a healthcare facility dedicated solely to the care of children and women. Arnold stepped up to the tee. With personal contributions and fund-raising efforts, he helped launch the Arnold Palmer Hospital for Children & Women in 1989, cutting the ribbon on his 60th birthday.

"Children's hospitals are not money makers, they are a service to the community," said John Bozard, head of Arnold Palmer Medical Center's Foundation. "Without the philanthropic support, and without him lending his name, and actually helping us make phone calls to potential donors to garner their support, this hospital would not have been in Orlando, Florida."

According to Orlando Health, a network of hospitals, Palmer believed "we can do better." In 2006, Arnold Palmer Hospital for Children & Women was transformed into two facilities. The Orlando Health Winnie Palmer Hospital for Women & Babies, with 315 beds, focused solely on women and babies. Meanwhile, the Arnold Palmer Medical Center, with 473 beds, became the largest facility in the country dedicated to the care of women and children.

In his lifetime Palmer donated more than $70 million to Orlando Health, and his giving didn't end there. For more than 40 years, he contributed to the March of Dimes. "From fundraisers on the golf course to speaking out for children with birth defects, Arnold Palmer is a champion for babies in every sense of the word," said Dr. Jennifer L. Howse, president of the March of Dimes. Palmer also formed the Arnie's Army Charitable Foundation, which invests in the well-being and development of children, supporting health and wellness initiatives and strengthening communities and the environment.

As chairman of the Latrobe Area Hospital Charitable Foundation, Palmer dreamt of building a cancer center in his hometown, so that patients and their families didn't have to drive to facilities in Pittsburgh. In 2002, the Arnold Palmer Pavilion, a cancer center in the Latrobe area, became

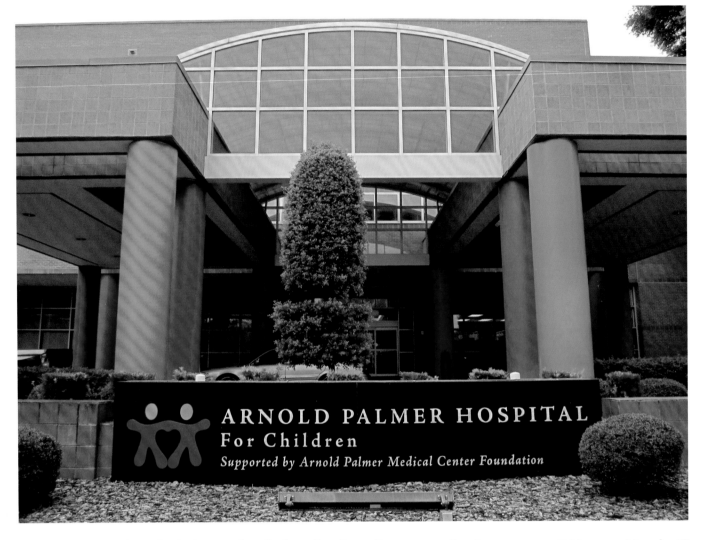

Arnold Palmer Hospital for Children, in Orlando, has been ranked as one of the nation's Top 30 pediatric hospitals for heart care and heart surgery by *U.S. News & World Report*. (Miosotis Jade, via Wikimedia Commons)

a reality. Also that year, Arnie's Army Battles Prostate Cancer was launched. More than 2,500 tournaments across the country, sponsored by the organization, have raised more than $3 million for prostate cancer research.

Upon Palmer's passing, Senate Majority Leader Harry Reid recognized The King's philanthropic contributions. "Golf made you famous," he wrote, "but your tireless efforts to save lives, not your short game, will make you immortal."

CHAPTER 9

LONG LIVE THE KING

On the Wednesday of Masters week in 2004, golfer Davis Love III noticed an old man by himself on Augusta's practice range. "Are you going to play?" Love asked. The old-timer, whom Love recognized as Arnold Palmer—who used to play with Davis Love Jr. back in the day—said that the golfer he was supposed to play with was not around. "Well," Love said, "you can play with me."

"He's been good to me since I was a very small child," Love said, "so it was an honor to get to play with him in his last Masters."

This was Arnold Palmer's 50th and final go-around at the Masters, and after charming Love with half-century-old stories about his father, he bore down on Thursday and shot a damn good 84. The next day, the 74-year-old shot the same score as the day before, then spoke to the press.

"I'm not going to make a big, long speech today," Palmer said. "I'm through. I've had it. I'm done. Cooked. Washed up. Finished."

He smiled and laughed, and everyone did the same. Many fought back happy tears, which became the typi-

Palmer bows to the gallery on the 6th green at Augusta National on Friday, April 9, 2004—his last-ever round at the Masters. Arnie played in 50 Masters, all consecutive. His four victories in the event set the record, but he did not crack the top 10 there after 1967. (AP Photo/ Amy Sancetta)

cal response throughout the legend's later years. On that special day, Arnold's two daughters, Peggy and Amy, were on hand, as were his four granddaughters and two grandsons. "That's never happened before at any golf tournament," he said. "So that was very special to me, to have them all here."

The only one missing was Winnie. Five years earlier in 1999, Arnold's wife of nearly 45 years passed away from cancer at age 65. Arnie and family were among the multitudes who had mourned her loss. Just two months before her death, Winnie called her friend Barbara Nicklaus, Jack's wife, with concerns about the Nicklauses' safety due to the upcoming Hurricane Floyd. "She was having difficulty breathing because of her illness, but she took the time to call," Barbara wrote in *Sports Illustrated*. The Metropolitan Golf Writers Association instituted the Winnie Palmer Award for "an individual in golf who has consistently given their time, energy and enthusiasm to those less fortunate."

In 2005 the widower remarried, exchanging vows with Kathleen "Kit" Gawthrop in a beach cottage in Hawaii. They had known each other for a while but married on a whim. "The minister, the bride, and the groom. That was it," Palmer said.

"What he'd went through with Winnie, and to find Kit, the love he's got with her now, it really helped him tremendously," said Hollis Cavner, director of the Champions Tour's 3M Championship. "She was absolutely the perfect thing for Arnold to get him back to being the Arnold we know and love."

***

On the links, the 1990s had been about milestones for Arnie. In 1993, he made the cut with a 73-76 at the Nestle Invitational—a phenomenal achievement for a 63-year-old. The $1,970 check for finishing 71st meant nothing compared to the pride that beamed within him. It was the 574th and final cut that he'd made on the PGA Tour.

> **"If it wasn't for Arnold Palmer, we wouldn't be playing for these obscene amounts of money we play for every week." —Rory McIlroy**

A year later Palmer made his final appearance in the U.S. Open, at Oakmont, 30 miles from his hometown of Latrobe. It came during a particularly eventful sports week. O. J. Simpson was on the run after allegedly killing his wife. New Yorkers were excited about the Rangers' appearance in the Stanley Cup Finals (against Vancouver) and the Knicks' in the NBA Finals (versus Houston). And the FIFA World Cup debuted on U.S. soil. At Oakmont during his final round, the attention was focused on Palmer, who teared up during the raucous ovations on the 18th hole. In the press tent afterward, he wept.

"It's been forty years of fun, work, and enjoyment," he said, wiping tears with a towel. "I haven't won all that much. I won a few tournaments. I won some majors. I suppose the most important thing . . ." He choked up. ". . . is the fact it's been as good as it's been to me."

He couldn't continue, but words were no longer necessary. In a rare display, the reporters set aside their journalistic oaths and gave The King a standing ovation.

More final appearances followed—the PGA Championship that summer and the British Open in 1995, at the most hallowed of golf shrines, St. Andrews. "As I was coming up 18, I kept thinking about 1960 and what it led to," Palmer said after his final round, his voice breaking. "A lot of great years and a lot of happy times." He noted that even though he had won the Masters and U.S. Open in 1960, he still had to qualify for the British Open that year. "I tell the young players that and they don't believe it," he said. "They don't think Arnold Palmer had to qualify for any tournament."

Arnie captained the U.S. Presidents Cup team in 1996, howling in delight when Fred Couples clinched the closely contested event with a long putt. A year later he faced his mortality for the first time, as he was diagnosed with prostate cancer. Successful surgery followed, and he went on to become a strong advocate of programs that supported cancer research and early detection. Lives, undoubtedly, were saved thanks to Arnie.

In 1999, Palmer was among a group of four "celebrity" investors who purchased Pebble Beach Golf Links, the most famous American course west of Augusta National. Palmer, actor/director Clint Eastwood, former Major League Baseball Commissioner Peter Ueberroth, and former United Airlines CEO Richard Ferris—along with a multitude of limited partners—purchased Pebble Beach for $820 million. It was a far cry from the five cents that Arnold had charged for hitting golf balls over the drainage ditch at Latrobe during his youth.

In 1999, the Westmoreland County Airport in Latrobe was renamed Arnold Palmer Regional Airport. He received many similar honors in his later years; 13 streets were named after him in the United States, and multiple Arnold Palmer statues were unveiled. In 2001, he proved more than just a museum piece, becoming just the third player in PGA Tour history to shoot his age, carding a 71 in the fourth round of the Bob Hope Chrysler Classic. Fans were giddy afterward, while Palmer groused over his double bogey on 16: "That should have been a birdie hole. If I make par there, I shoot 69 or maybe even 68."

In old age, Palmer remained relevant. He wore pink before it became "acceptable" for men to do so. In 2010, *Esquire* named him one of the "75 Best Dressed Men of All Time." He gave supermodel Kate Upton her first golf lesson, and in 2013 he rode into a Wake Forest football game on the back of a motorcycle. A few more tidbits, courtesy of the *Orlando Sentinel*: He led the campaign to prevent golf courses from being built in Florida's state parks. His grandkids called him "Dumpy." He owned more than 10,000 golf clubs. He loved bologna and Rolling Rock beer, produced by the Latrobe Brewing Company. And he had a dog named Mulligan that he walked at Bay Hill.

***

On the all-time list of PGA Tour wins, Palmer ranks fifth with 62, trailing Sam Snead (82), Tiger Woods (76), Jack Nicklaus (73), and Ben Hogan (64). In 2016,

At age 84, Arnold roars into the BB&T Field prior to a Wake Forest football game on October 19, 2013. Earlier in the week, the school unveiled a statue of their famous alum. (AP Images/ Chuck Burton)

Athlonsports.com rated the greatest golfers of all-time as 1) Woods, 2) Nicklaus, 3) Snead, 4) Palmer, and 5) Hogan.

Palmer was not just a golfer, but a national treasure. He is the only athlete to be presented with the Presidential Medal of Freedom (awarded in 2004) and Congressional Gold Medal (awarded in 2009, presented in 2012). At the Gold Medal ceremony, an emotional John Boehner said,

"Arnold Palmer democratized golf, made us think that we too could go out and play. Made us think that we could really do anything, really. All we had to do was to go out and try."

***

On September 22, 2016, Arnold Palmer was admitted to the University of Pittsburgh Medical Center to undergo testing

House Speaker John Boehner (R-OH), left, and Senate Majority Leader Harry Reid (D-NV), right, could finally agree on something: that Arnold Palmer was worthy of the Congressional Gold Medal, bestowed here on September 12, 2012. Boehner was moved to tears during the presentation. (AP Photo/J. Scott Applewhite)

on his heart. Heart surgery was scheduled, but he never made it. On Sunday, September 25, he passed, at the age of 87.

Soon, tributes poured in from around the world. Jack Nicklaus wrote, "We were great competitors, who loved competing against each other, but we were always great friends along the way. Arnold always had my back, and I had his. We were always there for each other. That never changed. He was the king of our sport and always will be."

> **"He had that other thing. The incredible ability to make you feel good—not just about him, but about yourself. He took energy from that and then turned around and gave it right back."**
> **—PGA Tour Commissioner Tim Finchem**

President Obama stated that Arnold "poured everything he had into everything he did: from building hospitals to personally responding to countless letters from his fans. And he did it all with a grin that hinted maybe he had one more shot up his sleeve. Today, Michelle and I stand with Arnie's Army in saluting the King."

On September 29, a private ceremony for Arnold was held in his hometown, with his ashes spread over Latrobe Country Club. On a cool, sunny morning on October 4, a public memorial service was held at St. Vincent College in Latrobe. A thousand people filled the basilica, and

5,000 more watched the ceremony via closed circuit at other locations on campus. A who's who of the golfing world attended, from Lee Trevino to Phil Mickelson, and Jack Nicklaus was among the speakers. "Don't be sad that it's over," Nicklaus said, quoting Vin Scully. "Smile because it happened." At one point in the service, Vince Gill brought the gathering to tears with his rendition of "You've Got a Friend."

Sam Saunders, Arnie's grandson, who caddied for him at his 50th Masters, delivered the most personal remarks. He recalled his phone conversation with his grandfather at 4:10 p.m. on Sunday, just hours before he died. "He asked me

The Youngstown Volunteer Fire Department, near the Latrobe Country Club, expresses its sentiment following Palmer's passing on September 25, 2016. (AP Photo/Gene J. Puskar)

Country singer Vince Gill played "You've Got a Friend" at the memorial service. "This man was my favorite person…that I ever met," an emotional Gill said. The performance can be seen on YouTube. (AP Images/Gene J. Puskar)

where I was," Sam recalled. "I said, 'I'm here at home. I'm thinking about you today—we all are.' He told me to take care of my babies and my entire family. I told him I loved him, and he told me he loved me back. It was the last thing we said to each other, and I will be grateful for that the rest of my life."

ARNIE BY THE NUMBERS

Arnold Palmer, a seven-time major winner, was a champion both on and off the course. (AP Photo)

PGA Tour Summary

Year	Starts	Wins	Top 10	Top 25	Cuts made	Earnings
1949	1	0	0	0	1	$0
1953	2	0	0	0	1	$0
1954	5	0	1	3	4	$0
1955	30	1	8	15	26	$7,958
1956	29	2	8	13	28	$16,145
1957	31	4	13	20	28	$27,803
1958	32	3	14	23	30	$42,608
1959	31	3	16	25	31	$32,462
1960	27	8	19	24	26	$75,263
1961	25	6	20	23	24	$61,091
1962	21	8	13	19	21	$81,448
1963	20	7	14	16	20	$128,230
1964	26	2	18	24	26	$113,203
1965	21	1	6	13	19	$57,771
1966	21	3	13	15	21	$110,468
1967	25	4	16	19	22	$184,065
1968	23	2	8	13	20	$87,496
1969	26	2	10	16	25	$95,267
1970	22	1	11	14	22	$100,941
1971	24	4	10	20	24	$162,896
1972	22	0	10	15	19	$81,440
1973	22	1	7	15	20	$87,275
1974	20	0	2	7	14	$32,627
1975	20	0	5	12	16	$59,018

Year	Starts	Wins	Top 10	Top 25	Cuts made	Earnings
1976	19	0	0	6	14	$17,018
1977	21	0	0	7	17	$21,950
1978	15	0	2	4	11	$27,073
1979	16	0	0	1	9	$9,276
1980	14	0	0	3	10	$16,589
1981	13	0	0	0	7	$4,164
1982	11	0	0	1	4	$6,621
1983	11	0	1	1	6	$16,904
1984	8	0	0	0	2	$2,452
1985	6	0	0	0	2	$3,327
1986	6	0	0	0	0	$0
1987	4	0	0	0	1	$1,650
1988	5	0	0	0	0	$0
1989	4	0	0	0	1	$2,290
1990	4	0	0	0	0	$0
1991	5	0	0	1	1	$7,738
1992	5	0	0	0	0	$0
1993	5	0	0	0	1	$1,970
1994	6	0	0	0	0	$0
1995	5	0	0	0	0	$0
1996	3	0	0	0	0	$0
1997	2	0	0	0	0	$0
1998	3	0	0	0	0	$0
1999	3	0	0	0	0	$0
2000	3	0	0	0	0	$0

Year	Starts	Wins	Top 10	Top 25	Cuts made	Earnings
2001	4	0	0	0	0	$0
2002	3	0	0	0	0	$0
2003	2	0	0	0	0	$0
2004	2	0	0	0	0	$0
TOTAL	**734**	**62**	**245**	**388**	**574**	**$1,784,497**

Arnold was the sole leader after all four rounds of the 1960 Masters and was the second wire-to-wire winner of the tournament. (AP Photo/Horace Cort)

Majors Summary

Tournament	Starts	Wins	Second	Third	Top 5	Top 10	Top 25	Cuts made
Masters	50	4	2	1	9	12	19	25
U.S. Open	33	1	4	1	10	13	18	24
British Open	23	2	1	0	3	7	12	17
PGA Championship	37	0	3	0	4	6	13	24

Majors Wins

Year	Championship	54 holes	Winning score	Margin	Runner(s)-up
1958	Masters Tournament	Tied for lead	−4 (70-73-68-73=284)	1 stroke	Doug Ford, Fred Hawkins
1960	Masters Tournament	1-shot lead	−6 (67-73-72-70=282)	1 stroke	Ken Venturi
1960	U.S. Open	7-shot deficit	−4 (72-71-72-65=280)	2 strokes	Jack Nicklaus (amateur)
1961	British Open	1-shot lead	−4 (70-73-69-72=284)	1 stroke	Dai Rees
1962	Masters Tournament	2-shot lead	−8 (70-66-69-75=280)	Playoff	Gary Player (2nd), Dow Finsterwald (3rd)
1962	British Open	5-shot lead	−12 (71-69-67-69=276)	6 strokes	Kel Nagle
1964	Masters Tournament	5-shot lead	−12 (69-68-69-70=276)	6 strokes	Dave Marr, Jack Nicklaus

Summary

Tournament	1953	1954	1955	1956	1957	1958	1959
Masters Tournament	DNP	DNP	T10	21	T7	1	3
U.S. Open	CUT	CUT	T21	7	CUT	T23	T5
British Open	DNP	DNP	DNP	DNP	DNP	DNP	DNP
PGA Championship	DNP	DNP	DNP	DNP	DNP	T40	T14

Tournament	1960	1961	1962	1963	1964	1965	1966	1967	1968	1969
Masters Tournament	1	T2	1	T9	1	T2	T4	4	CUT	27
U.S. Open	1	T14	2	T2	T5	CUT	2	2	59	T6
British Open	2	1	1	T26	DNP	16	T8	DNP	T10	DNP
PGA Championship	T7	T5	T17	T40	T2	T33	T6	T14	T2	WD

Tournament	1970	1971	1972	1973	1974	1975	1976	1977	1978	1979
Masters Tournament	T36	T18	T33	T24	T11	T13	CUT	T24	T37	CUT
U.S. Open	T54	T24	3	T4	T5	T9	T50	T19	CUT	T59
British Open	12	DNP	T7	T14	DNP	T16	T55	7	T34	DNP
PGA Championship	T2	T18	T16	CUT	T28	T33	T15	T19	CUT	CUT

Tournament	1980	1981	1982	1983	1984	1985	1986	1987	1988	1989
Masters Tournament	T24	CUT	47	T36	CUT	CUT	CUT	CUT	CUT	CUT
U.S. Open	63	CUT	CUT	T60	DNP	DNP	DNP	DNP	DNP	DNP
British Open	CUT	T23	T27	T56	CUT	DNP	DNP	CUT	DNP	CUT
PGA Championship	T72	76	CUT	T67	CUT	T65	CUT	T65	CUT	T63

Tournament	1990	1991	1992	1993	1994	1995	1996	1997	1998	1999
Masters Tournament	CUT	CUT	CUT	CUT	CUT	CUT	CUT	CUT	CUT	CUT
U.S. Open	DNP	DNP	DNP	DNP	CUT	DNP	DNP	DNP	DNP	DNP
British Open	CUT	DNP	DNP	DNP	DNP	CUT	DNP	DNP	DNP	DNP
PGA Championship	CUT	CUT	CUT	CUT	CUT	DNP	DNP	DNP	DNP	DNP

Tournament	2000	2001	2002	2003	2004
Masters Tournament	CUT	CUT	CUT	CUT	CUT
U.S. Open	DNP	DNP	DNP	DNP	DNP
British Open	DNP	DNP	DNP	DNP	DNP
PGA Championship	DNP	DNP	DNP	DNP	DNP

- DNP = Did not play
- WD = Withdrew
- CUT = missed the halfway cut
- "T" indicates a tie for a place

PGA SENIOR TOUR by the Numbers

- Victories—10.
- Last victory—1988 Crestar Classic.
- Majors played: 50.
- Majors won: 5 (PGA Seniors Championship—1980, 1984; U.S. Senior Open—1981; Senior Players Championship—1984, 1985).
- Top 10 in majors: 14 (PGA Seniors Championship—1980–82, 1984, 1988; U.S. Senior Open—1981–82, 1984; Senior Players Championship—1983–87, 1989).
- Top 5 in majors: 13 (PGA Seniors Championship—1980–82, 1984, 1988; U.S. Senior Open—1981, 1984; Senior Players Championship—1983–87, 1989).
- Career earnings: $1,677,342.

Senior PGA Tour Wins

No.	Date	Tournament	Winning score	Margin of victory	Runner(s)-up
1	Dec 7, 1980	PGA Seniors Championship	+1 (72-69-73-75=289)	Playoff	Paul Harney
2	Jul 12, 1981	U.S. Senior Open	+9 (72-76-68-73=289)	Playoff	Billy Casper, Bob Stone

No.	Date	Tournament	Winning score	Margin of victory	Runner(s)-up
3	Jun 13, 1982	Marlboro Classic	−8 (68-70-69-69=276)	4 strokes	Billy Casper, Bob Rosburg
4	Aug 15, 1982	Denver Post Champions of Golf	−5 (68-67-73-67=275)	1 stroke	Bob Goalby
5	Dec 4, 1983	Boca Grove Seniors Classic	−17 (65-69-70-67=271)	3 strokes	Billy Casper
6	Jan 22, 1984	General Foods PGA Seniors' Championship	−12 (66-66-72=204)	2 strokes	Don January
7	Jun 24, 1984	Senior Tournament Players Championship	−6 (69-63-79-71=282)	3 strokes	Peter Thomson
8	Dec 2, 1984	Quadel Seniors Classic	−11 (67-71-67=205)	1 stroke	Lee Elder, Orville Moody
9	Jun 23, 1985	Senior Tournament Players Championship	−14 (67-71-68-68=274)	11 strokes	Miller Barber, Lee Elder, Gene Littler, Charles Owens
10	Sep 18, 1988	Crestar Classic	−13 (65-68-70=203)	4 strokes	Lee Elder, Jim Ferree, Larry Mowry

PGA Tour by the Numbers

- Majors played: 123.
- Majors won: 7 (Masters—1958, 1960, 1962, 1964; British Open—1961, 1962; U.S. Open—1960).
- Times finished second: 10 (Masters—1961, 1965; British Open—1960; U.S. Open—1962, 1963, 1966, 1967; PGA Championship—1964, 1968, 1970).
- Missed Cut: 34.
- Top 10 in majors: 38 (Masters—1955, 1957–67; U.S. Open—1956, 1959–60, 1962–64, 1966–67, 1969, 1972–75; British Open—1960–62, 1966, 1968, 1972, 1977; PGA Championship—1960–61, 1964, 1966, 1968, 1970).

- Top 5 in majors: 26 (Masters—1958–62, 1964–67; U.S. Open—1959–60, 1962–64, 1966–67, 1972–74; British Open—1960–62); PGA Championship—1961, 1964, 1968, 1970).
- Last PGA Tour victory: 1973 Bob Hope Desert Classic.
- Career earnings: $1,861,857.

PGA Tour Wins by Name

1955 (1)

1. Canadian Open

1956 (2)

2. Insurance City Open
3. Eastern Open

1957 (4)

4. Houston Open
5. Azalea Open Invitational
6. Rubber City Open Invitational
7. San Diego Open Invitational

1958 (3)

8. St. Petersburg Open Invitational
9. Masters Tournament (major)
10. Pepsi Championship

1959 (3)

11. Thunderbird Invitational
12. Oklahoma City Open Invitational
13. West Palm Beach Open Invitational

1960 (8)

14. Palm Springs Desert Golf Classic
15. Texas Open Invitational
16. Baton Rouge Open Invitational
17. Pensacola Open Invitational
18. Masters Tournament (major)
19. U.S. Open (major)
20. Insurance City Open Invitational
21. Mobile Sertoma Open Invitational

1961 (6)

22. San Diego Open Invitational
23. Phoenix Open Invitational
24. Baton Rouge Open Invitational
25. Texas Open Invitational
26. Western Open
27. British Open (major)

1962 (8)

28. Palm Springs Golf Classic
29. Phoenix Open Invitational
30. Masters Tournament (major)
31. Texas Open Invitational
32. Tournament of Champions
33. Colonial National Invitation
34. British Open (major)
35. American Golf Classic

1963 (7)

36. Los Angeles Open
37. Phoenix Open Invitational

Arnold escapes from a sand trap near the 10th green at Indian Wells Country Club during the opening round at the 1973 Bob Hope Desert Golf Classic in Palm Springs, California. (AP Photo)

Arnie hoists the hardware after defeating Johnny Pott in an 18-hole playoff to win the Colonial tournament in Fort Worth, Texas, on May 14, 1962. (AP Photo/Ferd Kaufman)

38. Pensacola Open Invitational
39. Thunderbird Classic Invitational
40. Cleveland Open Invitational
41. Western Open
42. Whitemarsh Open Invitational

1964 (2)

43. Masters Tournament (major)
44. Oklahoma City Open Invitational

1965 (1)

45. Tournament of Champions

1966 (3)

46. Los Angeles Open
47. Tournament of Champions
48. Houston Champions International

1967 (4)

49. Los Angeles Open
50. Tucson Open Invitational
51. American Golf Classic
52. Thunderbird Classic

1968 (2)

53. Bob Hope Desert Classic
54. Kemper Open

1969 (2)

55. Heritage Golf Classic
56. Danny Thomas-Diplomat Classic

1970 (1)

57. National Four-Ball Championship (with Jack Nicklaus)

1971 (4)

58. Bob Hope Desert Classic
59. Florida Citrus Invitational
60. Westchester Classic
61. National Team Championship (with Jack Nicklaus)

1973 (1)

62. Bob Hope Desert Classic

With a lie too close to a tree to be played conventionally, Arnold hits a left-handed chip shot using a 6-iron during the 1959 PGA Championship at the Minneapolis Golf Course. He finished tied for 14th place. (AP Photo)

Misc. Awards and Honors

- Member, World Golf Hall of Fame
- PGA Tour money leader, 1958, 1960, 1962, 1963
- PGA Vardon Trophy (low scoring average) winner, 1961, 1962, 1964, 1967

- PGA Tour Player of the Year, 1960, 1962
- Member, U.S. Ryder Cup team, 1961, 1963, 1965, 1967, 1971, 1973
- Captain, U.S. Ryder Cup team, 1963, 1975
- Captain, U.S. Presidents Cup team, 1996

A fan adds his name to the hundreds of others who paid tribute to Mr. Palmer at the Ryder Cup at Hazeltine National Golf Club in Chaska, Minnesota, on September 28, 2016. (AP Photo/ Charlie Riedel)

BIBLIOGRAPHY

Books

Barclay, James. A. *Golf in Canada: A History.* Toronto: McClelland & Stewart, 1992.

Bender, Mike, with Michael Mercer. *Golf's 8 Second Secret.* Juno Beach, FL: Lawless Publishing, 2016.

Futterman, Matthew. *Players: The Story of Sports and Money, and the Visionaries Who Fought to Create a Revolution.* New York: Simon & Schuster, 2016.

Hauser, Thomas, with Arnold Palmer. *Arnold Palmer: A Personal Journey.* New York: NBC Publishing, 2012.

O'Connor, Ian. *Arnie & Jack: Palmer, Nicklaus, and Golf's Greatest Rivalry.* New York: Houghton Mifflin, 2008.

Palmer, Arnold, with James Dodson. *A Golfer's Life.* New York: Ballantine Books, 1999.

Palmer, Arnold, with Steve Eubanks. *Playing by the Rules.* New York: Atria Books, 2004.

Palmer, Arnold. *A Life Well Played: My Stories.* New York: St. Martin's Press, 2016.

Sounes, Howard. *The Wicked Game.* New York: William Morrow, 2004.

Venturi, Ken, with Michael Arkush. *Getting Up & Down: My 60 Years in Golf.* Chicago: Triumph Books, 2006.

Periodicals and Websites

ArnoldPalmer.com

Athlonsports.com

ESPN.com

Forbes.com

Golf.com

GolfChannel.com

GolfDigest.com

Golfweek.com

Los Angeles Times

New York Times

PGATour.com

Pittsburgh Post-Gazette

Saturday Evening Post

Sports Illustrated

USA Today

YouTube.com